Modelling
Further Aspects
of the
Coal Industry

Rob Johnson

BOOK LAW PUBLICATIONS

British Railways meets National Coal Board. An everyday occurence at Williamsthorpe Colliery in the days of the Nationalised industries, at least during the steam era. It is 8th March 1967 and these engines are enjoying a new lease of life whilst on loan to the NCB. There were about six engines, five Jinties and a J94, all based at Westhouses shed for these duties. Notice the tarpaulin on the front of the footplate of 47313 with a can or similar item close by. Both engines, the other is 47289, appear to have the crumpled sheet covering something or other. Who knows what lay within the confines of the lineside hut sporting the roughly hand painted KEEP OUT legend by the doorway - no matter - its an easy building to model, even scratchbuilt and the scrawl adds to the character. Notice the crossover beneath the wheels of 47313, quite an unusual piece of trackwork for a colliery yard. *M.J.Castledine.*

First published in the United Kingdom by
Book Law Publication
382 Carlton Hill, Nottingham, NG4 1JA
Printed and bound by The Amadeus Press, Cleckheaton, West Yorkshire.

INTRODUCTION

This second offering of *Modelling Aspects of the Coal Industry* is appropriately titled, as before, but with the addition of the adjective *Further*. Much of the additional material which makes up this volume has been made a available through the good offices of a number of people who are acknowledged elsewhere in the book. Suffice to say, their contribution has given me enough to illustrate an important section in this volume which was missing in the first volume - the models.

The first volume was well received and many letters of encouragement, besides telephone conversations, and personal meetings, confirmed both the publisher's and my own belief that such a book was required to point modellers in the right direction concerning the modelling of such an important section of our industrial history. Putting that first book together was both an enjoyable and enlightening experience and, not having gone into print before, it was somewhat foreboding to think that I might be able to help experienced modellers to 'have a go' creating an industrial diorama or suchlike where previously they may have only modelled structures directly associated with the running of the railway and its infrastructure.

Having 'taken the plunge' I was now well and truly 'hooked'. So, this offering, though similar to the previous book, has some new chapters taking the place of some of the earlier specifics. Whereas, in the first volume, seaborne related coal traffic was given a big 'splash', in this tome only one page is given to waterborne coal and that is set on a canal side in Lancashire, alongside a colliery, where the loading facilities were somewhat less spectacular and therefore easier to model.

What is vastly different in this book, compared to my previous effort, is the inclusion of illustrations showing actual models. Headframes and their associated buildings, locomotives, wagons and much more. These illustrations have been supplied by a small band of people who I approached 'out of the blue' and to whom I am extremely thankful for their immediate and positive response. The pictures certainly enhance the volume and help give a bit more credibility to a certain word found within the title of the book.

Also included this time are a number of 'adverts' found in the latter pages. These have been added so that you may inspect some of what the manufacturers and suppliers have on offer regarding coal related items. Many of the manufacturers - most of them being one or two man/woman operations - associated with the model railway industry require your input as to what you would like to see made available to make life easier for the railway modeller so why not drop them a line with your ideas. Remember that these people are extremely busy so don't expect a reply or acknowledgement and if you do not forget the s.a.e. Of course there are the electronic means of contact and websites are usually available nowadays.

As alluded to previously, the Somerset coalfield and its near neighbour set in the Forest of Dean, offer a great many examples of the smaller colliery which would make manageable model coal mines. Reference to late 20th century 25 inch scale Ordnance Survey maps will tell you instantly if a prototype would fit into your available space with little or no contraction or drastic changes. There are many excellent illustrated books on the market which show the railway and coal mine combination, usually in a picturesque rural setting.

Radstock comes to mind now because, within a very small area, the tiny Somerset town had, up to 1910, three collieries, a couple of wagon works, a very interesting triangular main line railway layout, all served by two main line railways with their own engine sheds and goods facilities - the Somerset & Dorset and the Great Western. Update to the Grouping period and you still have the two companies vying for the traffic. Jump into the 1950's and not much has changed except liveries and a slight drop in traffic levels. Nevertheless, that one town offers a great opportunity to model the LMS and GWR alongside each other with coal mines and wagons galore. It is a chance to run your 9F on a three or four coach 'stopper' whilst an ancient Pannier tank struggles to shunt twenty-odd loaded mineral wagons.

Even a simple exchange siding, with a branch going off through a tunnel, can give the impression of a coal mine being somewhere on the layout but sited some distance from and out of sight of the main line. A small engine shed, or stabling point, at the exchange sidings is an excuse to have an industrial locomotive on your layout. The possibilities are - as latterly coined in a recycling advertisement - endless.

Robert Johnson

This was the No.1 shaft headframe at Kirkby Colliery in the NCB's East Midland's Division in May 1966. Note that the construction appears to be a mixture of lattice and rolled steel girders. However, the four main legs are constructed from lattice girders, with plating covering the two legs nearest the winding house. Most probably the original legs would all have been open lattice type and the plating was most likely an NCB addition to give further strength to the legs when heavier, higher capacity, cages or skips were introduced at sometime in the late 1950's or early 60's. Opened in 1887, by Vesting Day this colliery employed just over 1,500 men and was winding about 400,000 tons of saleable coal a year. Investment by the Coal Board saw the saleable tonnage rise to near the one million ton mark in the 1960's but closure, in 1968, meant the magic figure was never attained. Situated on the north side of Kirkby-in-Ashfield, the colliery was bounded by the former Midland line to the east, with the old Great Northern Leen Valley Extension on its west side. Though not apparent in this view, the mine was literally surrounded by railways. *H.A.Gamble.*

Coal Fact: The amount of coal consumed in Greater London in 1900 was 15,745,658 tons of which 7,742,269 tons was brought by rail, 7,987,905 by sea and 15,484 tons by canal. In 1937, a peak year, 22,327,000 tons were consumed and of that 7,061,000 tons arrived by rail, 53,000 tons by canal and 15,213,000 by coastal vessels. During the period 1914 to 1926 the railways carried the bulk of the coal with the figures for 1918 showing 10,122,122 tons by rail and only 3,533,185 by coaster. Much of the seaborne trade originated at the north-east ports (Blyth, Tees, Tyne and Wear).

Coal Fact: In 1956 British Railways estimated that the Eastern Region's originating coal class traffic employed approximately 120,000 wagons or 20% of the BR mineral wagon stock.

(left) Detail of the No.2 (Upcast) headframe at Astley Green Colliery, Lancashire, revealed during demolition of the pit head building in the 1970's - *see* later.

MORE COLLIERIES

This is Nostell Colliery near Wakefield just prior to World War One. The timber headframe of the downcast shaft can be seen to be completely surrounded by the screens and associated pit head buildings, all, note, of simple wooden construction. The winding house is typically brick built as is the boiler house with its six Lancashire boilers showing their faces to the yard. During its NCB ownership this mine was producing on average about a quarter of a million tons of saleable coal a year, a figure which would put it in the 'medium' size of colliery. Viewed from this angle, the layout appears to be compact enough to enable a scale model to be built in 4mm or smaller scale, without taking up vast tracts of valuable board space. Even when modernised with new steel headframes and a more permanent screens building, the mine managed to keep within the bounds of the old layout. Closure took place in 1987. Note the P.O. wagons, including one of the Nostell fleet, are all looking fairly weary even then. Although the horse and cart may well be regarded as period pieces, they were still in use up to the 1950's with private coalmen. *Authors collection.*

The screens at Cadley Hill Colliery consisted this steel framed, corrugated asbestos clad building. Modelling such a structure would be easy enough and unless you were going to model the prototype, it is possible to scale it down somewhat in order to make it fit the available space. There appears to be about twelve tracks beneath the screens but four or even three such tracks would look very authentic whilst still giving the illusion of a monumental building. Note the wagons, the nearest of which seem to be former BR 21-ton, double door coal wagons. besides the NCB markings, each has got the crudely painted initials CH with a fleet number alongside. Not forgetting the locomotive, this was RSH 7298, an 0-6-0ST of 1946. Painted in red livery, it carried the name PROGRESS and is now preserved at the Tanfield Railway. Cadley Hill was part of the South Derbyshire coalfield and was sunk in the 1860's. By the time of this 16th July 1970 photograph, it employed about four hundred men mining some 250,000 tons of coal a year. Situated a few miles south-east of Burton-upon-Trent, alongside the A444 road, it was connected to other nearby mines by way of an interesting double and single track railway system, centred on Swadlincote, which would hold up to further research and examination for a prototype background. *H.A.Gamble.*

Widdrington opencast was one of the more 'permanent' sites for this type of mining. Situated in Northumberland, the disposal point was just east of the East Coast Main Line with access to it. The opencast site, operated by Derek Crouch (Contractors), Ltd., was known as Radar North to the NCB and had seam names such as 'Little Wonder', 'Top and Main of Broomhill', 'Bottom' and Cheeveley'. In May 1970 exBR J94 No.68078, designated L2, was working the site and is seen here approaching the screening plant with a load of raw coal from the large open pit. In model form this particular plant would not present too much of a challenge and the finished piece would look extremely impressive. This whole group of buildings was constructed on stilts of various sizes and the whole lot was clad in corrugated materials. All the rolled steel columns, joists and corrugation are available in model form for scratchbuilding from the likes of Plastruct FineLine or Evergreen. Note the 'added-on' effect of some of the structures which is one of the beauties of modelling coal related industry. You can simply add on another piece whenever you feel the need to expand or enhance the model further. *Malcolm Castledine.*

Under the 'screens' at Brodsworth Colliery in 1955, with 21-ton Loco Coal wagons being loaded. The loading conveyor is just visible and is nearing the end of its work at this end of the wagon and a slight nudge will be required to move the 21-tonner further along to complete loading. The supporting columns here are concrete, cast in situ. Note the limited clearance once these wagons are full. You can understand why the 24$\frac{1}{2}$-ton wagons needed the older 'screens' to be altered somewhat. Luckily for the photographer the wagon is newly painted and reflects the flash from the camera, otherwise the murk and pathetic illumination would not reveal a lot! *Bill Johnson coll.*

(opposite) When Astley Green Colliery became part of the Manchester Collieries group in 1929, a new washery was erected at the eastern end of the yard to accept coal from the likes of Mosley Common mine which was linked to Astley Green by a new standard gauge railway from Boothstown. The new washery had four loading roads and one spoil road, besides all the associated water 'purifying' plant. Loaded wagons were parked in these dead-end sidings prior to collection. This 1936 view of the plant has the wagons on the left appearing to contain dirt whilst the others have different grades of small coal. Note the ends of the wagons all carry the Manchester Collieries 'M' logo; the full title of the company graced the sides of the vehicles.

Although the subject of this photograph is the red liveried Hawthorn Leslie 0-6-0ST HL3534 of 1922, NCB No.S115, named FRANK, this April 1970 view shows some interesting architecture at Wheldale Colliery in Yorkshire. The enclosed conveyor housings and walkways are basically steel framed with brick in-fill cladding and, they are going off at different angles and gradients. Note also the closeness of other buildings and the apparent random fixing of cables. *H.A.Gamble.*

Modernisation of the 'landsale' facility at West Riding Colliery in the late 1920's brought this steel framed bunker equipped with six hoppers for the use of coal merchants. The brick infill walls of the bunker are typical of the period when 'screens' were being erected using the same materials. *Authors collection.*

Coal Fact: MGR. Once built the new overhead loading bunkers could cause their own problems as was the case at Sharlston Colliery, Yorkshire in January 1969. During loading operations of an MGR train, bound for Ferrybridge power station, the bunker collapsed giving very little warning to the men working beneath at the time. Luckily the men escaped the collapse but three HAA wagons of a train being loaded were trapped beneath an estimated 1,500 tons of coal and the associated steelwork of the bunker. An old mine shaft, which was not shown on plans and not found during preliminary boring prior to erection of the bunker, was apparently the cause of the collapse. Built in 1968, the bunker had a capacity of 3,000 tons and cost some £350,000 and had been in commission just eight months. The buried HAA wagons were written-off.

An overhead view of the demolition of No.2 headframe at Astley Green Colliery revealing further 'all round' detail in the colliery. Note the amount of and the positioning of the various pipework.

This view at Grimethorpe Colliery in April 1971 is included to show the construction and cladding of the conveyor housing in this section of the mine. The framework is made up from rolled steel in varying sections, L and H in the main. Cladding consists of corrugated asbestos both on the sides and curved roof sections. Dominating the background are the ventilation shafts which by now sent power assisted fresh air into the mine and needed massive concrete ducting as here. Laid aside and redundant is 0-6-0ST No.4, a Vulcan Foundry 1945 build No.5295, and was ex WD 75305. The engine had been rebuilt with a Hunslet underfeed stoker but in 1972 No.4 was scrapped. Note the newly acquired large headlight on the front of the tank. *H.A.Gamble.*

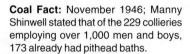

Coal Fact: November 1946; Manny Shinwell stated that of the 229 collieries employing over 1,000 men and boys, 173 already had pithead baths.

Coal Fact: Tunnel drivages in NCB mines during 1979 amounted to 482 kilometres. In 1980 - 527 kilometres. 1981 - 548 kilometres. Each of those years amounted to more than the entire length of tunnels on the London Underground system.

The western end of Pye Hill Colliery yard in May 1964, showing the 'main line' with one of the pit's three Andrew Barclay outside cylinder 0-4-0ST's making its way to the engine shed seen on the right. This partial view of the yard gives us further detail to consider for inclusion on the colliery section of our layout. Amongst the more permanent features is the row of terraced housing backing onto one of the colliery sidings; no doubt these houses were occupied by employees of the colliery. Concrete street lamps with elegant swan necks (quite a change from the austere designs normally found) grace the 'main line' as though it was a public road. The sleepered road crossing, with its dirt covering, gives an indication of where road vehicles might venture. Mobile detail includes the Ruston Bucyrus RB-22 drag line excavator and, on the right, the period Morris van. Note the gentle curves on this layout, the trackwork is in various states, leading down to the overbridge which carried the Great Northern line Codnor Park to Pinxton. Beyond that, on the same level as the colliery yard, is the former Midland Railway Erewash Valley main line. Pye Hill Colliery was opened in 1875 and became one of the later closures in this part of the Notts/Derby coalfield. Its six hundred strong workforce brought more than a quarter of a million tons of coal to the surface each year during the period of nationalisation. *R.C.Riley.*

Wath marshalling yard or to be more precise the south end arrival sidings of that yard in the summer of 1954. The principal aim of this installation was to marshal and dispatch coal from the south Yorkshire collieries to the hungry mills, factories and industrial concerns of south Lancashire and it had carried out that particular function since it was laid down and opened by the Great Central Railway in 1907. The upper of these two views, both of which were commissioned by BR, shows on the left a Robinson O4 which has just arrived on a coal train and is about to be uncoupled to make its way back to Mexborough shed or perhaps pick up a train of empties destined for a specific colliery. At this period Wath was taking in fifty-three coal trains a day from twenty-one collieries. The interesting part of the picture is the pair of double headed Darlington built 350 h.p. 0-6-0 diesel electric shunters, which are two of the five Wath based engines numbered 13060 to 13064 (later D3060 to D3064), which appear to be pushing a loaded train 'over the hump' and into the yard. The diesels had arrived at Wath in August of the previous year so these photographs probably had nothing to do with the 'new' motive power which had taken over the Wath yard shunting from the huge 0-8-2T S1's and, neither locomotive was in a pristine external condition. So, I think that the tandem working was either arranged to show the concept of the 'Master and Slave' units which were eventually built some eleven years later for use in the new Tinsley marshalling yard or perhaps it was arranged simply to show a 'staged' trip working. Anyway, it is not everyday that one gets the chance to see these shunting locomotives working in tandem, hence their inclusion in this album. So those of you who have a pair of these engines and operate an early or late BR period layout, or even modern image, then this type of working was not unusual - or was it? Most of us like to be prototypically correct so a trip working using a pair of these 350 h.p. shunters would not, it seems, be out of place. The lower picture gives an overall impression of Wath Central with the marshalling yard in the left background, spoil heaps dominate the centre and right background whilst the permanent way here has a distinct covering of coal dust. As for those two diesels, they now appear to be heading south on the main line with the same train. The average yearly total of coal wagons handled at Wath was 450,000 'fulls' and 200,000 'empties'. Other goods vehicles handled at the yard amounted to 25,000 'loaded' wagons with 20,000 'empties'. *British Railways.*

THE RAILWAYS - DELIVERING THE GOODS

With something like eight hundred tons pushing it westwards, O4/1 No.63743 nears Skelton Junction in 1954 with a load of south Yorkshire coal contained in 24½ ton wagons. The small coal would be for industrial use and it was probably bound for one of the public utilities in south-west Lancashire or north Cheshire. *J.Devonport.*

Here is an 0-6-2T with a heavy load at Craigentinny in the 1930s. This is another glimpse into prototype practice showing that medium powered tank engines were pressed into main line service by the LNER where conditions suited. There appears to be a locomotive at the rear of the train which may well have been on banking duties but most probably has just brought the train of empty mineral wagons, complete with N15, No.9910 of St Margarets shed bringing up the rear, from South Leith. Now having gained the main line the N15 has charge of the train which it will haul to one of the collieries situated on the west side of Edinburgh.

(above) For those of you who model the Annesley-Woodford 'Runners' with a BR 9F or Thompson O1 at the head, here is a nice alternative piece of motive power in the shape of V2 No.60847, formerly named ST.PETERS SCHOOL YORK. The date is 10th October 1964 and this particular coal traffic is in fast decline. With its once large fleet of 9F 2-10-0's being dispersed to depots all over the country, Annesley shed was using anything 'decent' it could get its hands on to haul these slick trains. With plenty of speed built up for the last part of the climb out of Nottingham, the York based V2 is noisily passing through the rock cutting at New Basford on the former GC main line through the northern suburbs of Nottingham with a Down empties working. Note that all the wagons are the 16-ton steel bodied mineral type, unfitted of course. *Malcolm Castledine.*

(below) Collett 2-8-0 No.3813 with a train of thirty-three loaded 20-ton and 21-ton steel bodied coal wagons at Bassaleg, Monmouthshire, in September 1945. The train appears to be heading westwards towards Machen and is probably bound for one of the coke ovens further along the line. Note the amount of weed growth covering the permanent way, no doubt wartime neglect was still prevalent. As an aside, this particular engine was one of twenty of the GWR Churchward/Collett 8F's to be converted to oil burning in the period between 1946 and 1949, during the so-called 'Coal Crisis' of the late 1940's. Once it was realised that coal supplies could be guaranteed all twenty quickly reverted to coal burning again. Whilst it was an oil burner, No.3813 was temporarily renumbered No.4855. *British Railways.*

13

(*above*) Regarding scale, this picture gives you a good idea of what a medium sized power station and its railway infrastructure would look like when married together in model form. The gigantic chimney is nearly as tall as the train is long and as for the generating building well they would probably fill the average room. I'm not going to mention cooling towers! So, the power station (customer) looks like a doubtful subject for modelling in the majority of cases. I apologise to anyone who purchased the first book and were led to believe that a power station was a decent subject to model at 4mm or above scale. As for 2mm and under, well perhaps but you are still pushing the bounds a bit. For the record, this is Uskmouth power station in October 1968 with a Class 37 arriving with a train of loaded 16-tonners. Eventually the train, less the locomotive, will enter the discharge building (on the extreme left) and the wagons will be tipped over through nearly 180 degrees, one-by-one - a slow laborious task which tied up thousands of wagons until the advent of the MGR. Uskmouth PS consisted two installations the nearest with the single chimney was commissioned in 1962 and could generate 336 megawatts. Behind is the 1956 built station which had a capacity of 342 megawatts. Combined, the two stations had the same capacity as one of the modern 660 megawatt turbine generating sets found in any of today's base load power stations.

(*below*) 'Under the wires' in the Sheffield area during the 1950's, a filthy Robinson O4/1 No.63889, of Darnall shed, has charge of a loaded coke train which has a brake van at both ends. Note that the hoppers are piled high above the front brake van and almost fill the loading gauge. Beyond stationery B1 No.61186 another O4/1 No.63664, from Langwith Junction depot, has charge of a coal train

Working out its last year of life, Sunderland based Q6 No.63395 drags a short train of empty 21-ton hoppers through Ryhope Junction and leaves the coastal route behind as it heads inland on the Stockton line in March 1967. Bound for one of the numerous collieries still operating in this area of County Durham, this was typical of the mineral trains found working the BR lines in north-east England. By this period diesels were well entrenched on the coal trains in this part of the country and the likes of English Electric Type 3 (Class 37), BR Sulzer Type 2 (Class 25), EE Type 1 (Class 20), and Clayton Type 1 (Class 17), could all be seen alongside the few remaining steam locomotives comprising J27's, Q6's, Ivatt Cl.4's and WD 2-8-0's. A layout featuring the transition years in NE England would therefore require very few locomotive classes to furnish it although we have not taken into account the various diesel shunters also found in the area at that time. As for the wagon stock, BR steel bodied hoppers presented in umpteen colour schemes and varying shades of rust and dirt, should do the trick. *(N.E.Stead collection)*

Perhaps the ultimate in British freight motive power, the LMS Beyer Garratt. This is No.4997 in September 1931 pulling out of the spur and rejoining the main line at Whitacre with a Toton to Birmingham coal train. The ensemble is made up of numerous P.O., LMS and GWR wagons of all sizes. No doubt the nineteen wagons on view constitute just a portion of the train but nevertheless it makes an impressive sight so there is no need to have extremely long trains to justify the use of one of these engines. In this view No.4997 has its original square fixed bunker but within a year or so it gained one of the rotary bunkers, albeit second-hand, from No.4986. *J.A.G.H.Coltas.*

J11 No.5950 seems to be making easy work of this long train of empty P.O. wagons on the Down slow at Corby Glen, en route from London to the East Midlands coalfield circa 1935. This Retford based engine will have brought this lot from New England having worked to Peterborough with an Up loaded train which probably was not quite as long as this entourage.

Another Retford based J11 on the GN Main line, this one with a loaded coal train on the Up main at Retford and bound for London via New England, on a summer evening circa 1938.

WD 2-10-0 No.90766 sorts out a train of empty steel and wooden bodied 16-ton mineral wagons at Grangemouth in April 1961. The ten-coupled version of the WD 'Austerity' 2-8-0 was confined to working virtually exclusively in the Scottish Region and except for a couple of examples based at the Caledonian's Carlisle shed at Kingmoor from time to time, the twenty-five strong class were based at former Caley depots in Scotland. Motherwell and Grangemouth sheds had the bulk of the class allocated and that was the position until withdrawal started in 1961. Within a year the class ceased to exist but scenes such as this remind us of the daily toil undertaken by the class moving coal around the Scottish coalfields. *G.M.Staddon, N.E.Stead coll.*

Royston engine shed, summer 1965, with two of the depot's recently acquired 4F 0-6-0's having a weekend break with the other inhabitants which comprised mainly Stanier 8F's at this time with a handful of WD 2-8-0's. Note the external state of all the engines on view - but this was the period in the age of steam when cleaners were thin on the ground and authority did not really encourage the cleaning of the rapidly dwindling steam locomotive fleet, especially coal haulers such as these. To reproduce this authentic grime is not too difficult but care must be taken not to over do it. Little bits of detail such as the chalked working code '8X47' or some other legend make for authenticity. Note the cab number on the adjacent WD is all but obliterated by dirt, a point which could be useful if you run a fleet of these 2-8-0's and haven't got round to numbering them all yet.

With plenty of steam to spare, O4 No.63601 drifts along the former Great Central route past Old Mill Lane signal box, Barnsley with a short (15-wagon) coal train in April 1961. The majority of the wagons are steel bodied 16-ton minerals with just a couple of wooden bodied examples thrown in for variety. Note the top of the tender which is full of coal of varying quality spread over all the horizontal surfaces, a feature rarely modelled but prototypically correct, at least for the 1960's. This coal movement would hardly tax the 2-8-0 but it looks right, especially working tender first. I'm not totally sure if this was a mine to yard run or a pick-up but either working would fit the bill.

Coal Fact: The 1949 Report & Accounts for BR show that the average coal load increased from 10.97 tons to 11.25 tons in December partly due to the increase in the number of 16-ton wagons and partly because of "better loading on the part of the NCB." The round trip time of wagons decreased from 8.34 days in January to 7.71 days in December. Terminal used time still approximated to just over two days.

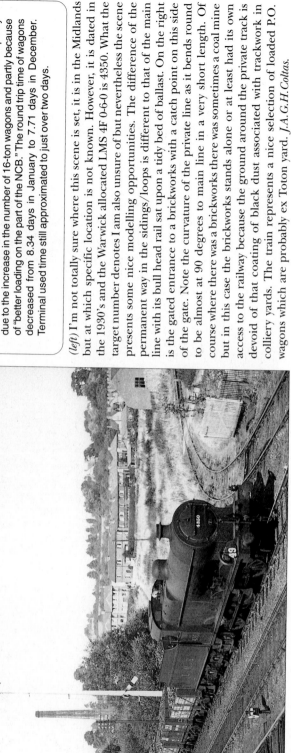

(left) I'm not totally sure where this scene is set, it is in the Midlands but at which specific location is not known. However, it is dated in the 1930's and the Warwick allocated LMS 4F 0-6-0 is 4350. What the target number denotes I am also unsure of but nevertheless the scene presents some nice modelling opportunities. The difference of the permanent way in the sidings/loops is different to that of the main line with its bull head rail sat upon a tidy bed of ballast. On the right is the gated entrance to a brickworks with a catch point on this side of the gate. Note the curvature of the private line as it bends round to be almost at 90 degrees to main line in a very short length. Of course where there was a brickworks there was sometimes a coal mine but in this case the brickworks stands alone or at least had its own access to the railway because the ground around the private track is devoid of that coating of black dust associated with trackwork in colliery yards. The train represents a nice selection of loaded P.O. wagons which are probably ex Toton yard. *J.A.G.H.Coltas.*

Wouldn't it be nice to have the room, rolling stock and funds to reproduce something like this in model form. Alas few, if any, of us have such resources at our disposal. However, the view of one of the Cardiff docks' reception yards reveals plenty of modelling ideas such as; where is the boundary between hand operated and signal controlled points? On this layout there does not seem to be any demarcation line between the two, which are visible everywhere. Note the point rodding curving round in the centre of the picture, it seemingly stretches into the distance from whence it came but where it has to cross the yard lines it burrows under the tracks and is covered between, especially where it changes direction by means of pulleys and levers. In the foreground more rodding goes off to the right between piles of old timbers and rail. The rodding is rarely modelled, even in a dummy inactive form but it helps bring more realism to a layout if this 'easy to produce' feature is applied. *Authors collection.*

The procession of coal trains on the ECML continued year round, only letting up during times of industrial dispute or interruptions due to severe weather conditions. In late May 1935, O2 No.3481 heads north along the Down slow line through Sandy with a train of mineral empties whilst, on the Up slow, a loaded train in the hands of another 2-8-0, heads for London.

Making its way home to Motherwell whilst en route from Alloa, WD 2-8-0 No.90386 has just crossed the other Forth railway bridge, built by the Caledonian Railway, which was situated at Throsk. Besides the coal load, the train includes a number of empty bogie bolster wagons bound for one of the Lanarkshire steelworks. Considering that the latter county had a number of coal mines still in operation when this scene was captured in the late 1950's, it makes one wonder why this train was carrying 'coals to Newcastle' so to speak but the fact was that some industrial concerns required a blend of different coals from other coalfields to mix with the local coal. Note the one time gated siding going off to the left. Although in this instance it was not a colliery branch, it could easily form the basis of one in model form, complete with signal, locking bars and slip point. To finish the scene, although out of picture in this view, there was a halt on the main line just behind the photographer.

Coal Fact: Opened July 1832, the Leicester & Swannington Rly had a 1¾ mile branch to a mine at Ibstock. The railway carried coals to Leicester and the branch was worked by horses. A year later steam locomotives took over as traffic grew. The mines produced coal until closed in 1929. The branch continued to serve local industry until 1957. Coal deposits in the area were later exploited when the NCB opened Bagworth Colliery.

Coal Fact: At the height of the BR Merry-Go-round era, the heaviest trains run on a daily basis were those which ran between Newstead Colliery, Nottinghamshire, to Staythorpe power station. Weighing in at 2341 tons, the train consisted 55 HAA hopper wagons with a payload of 1650 tons, all of it hauled by a single Class 47 diesel locomotive.

Here is a nice tidy train with Collett 0-6-2T No.5606 heading north with a long rake of empties at Hatton in 1938. Although unidentified, the wagons appear to have the same owner, at least the first dozen anyway. There are probably about fifty wagons in this train which may seem excessive for such an engine but these 0-6-2T's were rated 5MT by BR and they were empties'. *J.A.G.H.Coltas.*

Coking plants may not have the same attraction to modellers as the coal mines but there are exceptions amongst us who like to go for and model the more unusual aspects of the hobby. Besides the monolithic bulk of the coke ovens, with the associated and apparently myriad of pipework, the model would require something out of the ordinary in the way of motive power for the coke gondolas and the model trade has yet to come up with anything approaching the likes of this particular fireless beast which was employed at the Glasshoughton Coal Products Division plant. The frames, wheels and steam vessel (we can't use the term boiler because, strictly speaking, it didn't) were supplied as an 0-6-0F locomotive by Robert Stephenson & Hawthorns, No.8082 in 1958. As for the rest of the contraption - cab, ladders, shielding and control extensions - I believe it too was supplied by RS&H. Whatever its origin, it is different and very 'Heath Robinson' but it certainly did the job it was designed for. This Saturday 18th April 1970 group of pictures captured by the camera of a visiting Horace Gamble, shows the locomotive from various angles and hopefully the views will inspire someone to have a go. For those already showing some interest, its livery was blue and I think that included the cab. It was scrapped on site in November 1971.

Coal Fact: December 1925, Sir Ralph Wedgwood, Chief General Manager of the LNER told a Hearing of the Coal Commission that the railway industry had a double interest in the coal trade. To back up his claims he mentioned that the railways were very large consumers of coal and at the same time they are the main carriers of coal, coke and patent fuels with tonnage's equal to 84% (225 million tons) of the total output (267 million tons) of the coal mines. As consumers of coal the railway companies had a great interest in a low and stable price for coal and, during 1924 they used some 13.5 million tons (approximately 5% of output) in locomotives alone. The total tonnage of coal exported (including bunkering) in 1924 was 95.34 million tons of which the railway companies carried 85.17 million tons (89.3% of total) (LNER carried 41.5 million tons). Some 66.41 million tons of this tonnage was shipped through railway owned docks or at shipping places worked by them. The average length of haul in 1924 was exactly 44 miles. Of these figures, 69% was carried in private owner wagons and 31% in railway owned wagons.

Coal Fact: 18th June 1954; The first of the new coke oven plants brought into production since nationalisation of the coal industry was opened at Fishburn, County Durham.

INDUSTRIAL LOCOMOTIVES

Coal Fact: Hard to believe perhaps but opencast mining has been used in the reclamation process of former deep mining areas. One such opencast operation was on part of what became the Telford New Town site in the 1970's when 200 years of coal and iron mining, and clay extraction, had produced an area which was most unsuitable for anything else. However, opencast mining managed to remove 200 old shafts and 520 acres of derelict land was reclaimed for housing. Furthermore, nearly one and quarter million tons of coal was extracted and reclaimed during the clean-up.

(above) Seen from the overhead gantry apparent in the previous view, we get a look at the front ? end of the Fireless which reveals further detail. What material the cab was constructed from I am not sure, it was probably asbestos clad anyway no matter if it was steel or timber. Note the wooden sleepered track.

(left) Coke being discharged from one of the ovens into the waiting gondola. Trying to reproduce this in model form would be virtually impossible and as for all the smoke and obnoxious fumes! Anyway this picture is included to show a side of the coal industry rarely seen and certainly rarely experienced by most of us.

(below) Every now and then the Fireless locomotive required a top up with high pressure steam and here the connection is made. The driver, who has now vacated his cab, probably had one of the least attractive jobs in British industry - it makes smoking in the workplace seem suddenly more agreeable. With the discharge machine out of the way we can see the battery of ovens on the left. Back on the ground, note the four wheel front loader clearing up the spillage alongside the track beneath the large coke gondola.

Coal Fact: Opencast mining enabled coal seams as thin as 5 inches (130mm) to be worked, whereas in a deep mine, coal seams with a thickness less than 18 inches (460mm) were basically unworkable.

Coal Fact: The manufacture of coke oven by-products rose considerably between 1947 and 1956: pure benzole production rose from 17 to 31 million gallons a year during that period. Crude tar manufacture went from 320,000 tons in 1947 to 403,000 tons in 1956. NCB produced coke sales reached their highest in 1955 when nearly seven and a half millions tons of varying grades were sold for blast furnace, foundry, industrial and domestic use.

0-4-0 + 0-4-0 WILLIAM FRANCIS, perhaps the ultimate British industrial steam locomotive. Photographed at Baddesley Colliery, its home since delivery from Beyer, Peacock (No.6841) in 1937, this Garratt certainly looks the part on a rainy Saturday 21st August 1965. It is perhaps a shame that the cleaning rags had not been employed. After all, it was by then the only locomotive of its type still working in the British coalfields. Being a Saturday, the engine was having a break from its normal duties and was brought out so that the photographers could pay homage in their particular way. Besides this Warwickshire based Garratt, there was up to 1963 another similar engine working Sneyd Colliery at Burslem in Staffordshire, SNEYD COLLIERIES No.3, B.P. 6729 of 1931, but it was cut up on site when its working days were over. Luckily WILLIAM FRANCIS has been preserved at Bressingham. If such a locomotive was available in model form, it could perhaps push some of you into creating a purely industrial layout rather than a layout with an industrial setting alongside its main line, or sitting in that awkward corner. Food for thought? *H.A.Gamble.*

Former main line and later BR locomotives in the employ of the NCB or their contractors, has always been normal practice and had been throughout most of the 20th Century, even prior to 1923. When BR was getting rid of its steam motive power at an alarming rate during the 1960's, they sold quite a few to industry as a whole and to the NCB in particular. Besides the steam locomotives, there was of course all those redundant, and hardly run-in, diesel shunting and trip-working engines which the NCB swallowed up dozens at a time. This picture features former LMS 'Jinty' No.47445 (HE 1529/27) at Elsecar [Pepper's yard] screens on 16th April 1968. Withdrawn in April 1966 from Crewe South, the 0-6-0T was one of the few of its type purchased by the NCB although there was a number 'on loan' (*see* Williamthorpe Colliery). On the face of it the engine is quite unremarkable with little change to its former BR state except perhaps the missing handrail on the boiler and smokebox side. It even still wears the electrification warning flashes from its days in service at Crewe. But its livery had to be seen to be believed - Boiler black, Tanks orange, Frames red, Sandbox blue. Now that combination of colours, for a locomotive livery, might dissuade some people from indulging in an industrial diorama or feature on the layout but hold fire because the next picture could sway you back again. Finally, note the 'Jinty's' surroundings which consist of modern 'mobile' or semi permanent plant. *H.A.Gamble.*

Everybody knows about the ten Hawksworth GWR designed Heavy Pannier tanks introduced in 1949 and which then had a hard time finding suitable work in the contracting Western Region. Three of them, Nos.1501, 1502 and 1509, were bought by the NCB for work at Coventry Colliery and on 14th July 1966 No.1502 was captured on film at its new workplace. Note that although the smokebox numberplate has gone, the engine has managed to keep its brass cabside plates. A shunting pole appears on the running plate alongside a large can of lubricating oil. What seems to be the remnants of a spark arrester clings onto the right side of the chimney; I'm not sure if that piece of equipment was a necessary requirement of Coventry Colliery environs or perhaps it was a leftover from its last BR allocation. Of the three 0-6-0PT's, No.1501 was eventually preserved and is now on the Severn Valley, but the other two were broken up in 1970, probably as their boilers came up for renewal. To the left of the engine can be seen what appears to be an avenue of trees leading up to the headframes in the right background. The grass surrounding the trees looks to be well manicured - a scene which makes a nice change from the grime and rubbish strewn vistas normally associated with coal mines. *H.A.Gamble.*

So, you have not got the room on your layout for a coal mine or its diverse infrastructure but you do run trains so there is no reason not to have another aspect of the coal industry besides the coal trains. This Saturday 5th May 1962 scene, at Leicester Central South Goods yard, shows us two former MoS, and now ex WD 0-6-0ST's en route to NCB Yorkshire, their new owners. Both engines are Hunslet built and 71445, WD No.139 is works No.3209 of 1945. It went to Wharncliffe Woodmoor Colliery and was scrapped in 1968. No.75121 (which already appears in this book) was WD No.135 and HE 3171 of 1944. Note that no coupling rods are fitted - they would be in the bunker, in the cab or within the vans marshalled between the engines. However, except for the hook, there are no means of coupling the train to another wagon. Most probably the hauling locomotive would provide a screw coupling to make the connection nice and tight. Anyway, another avenue of ideas has been opened up so its now down to you. *H.A.Gamble.*

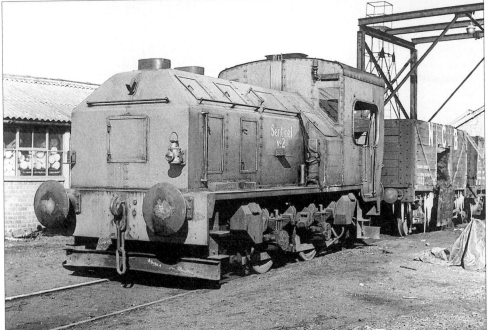

Steam Sentinel No.2, works No.9580 of 1954, resided at Ramcroft Colliery in Derbyshire. This Sunday, 8th March 1964 photograph shows the ten years old locomotive in a reasonable condition. The bright sunshine hides the fact that it was bitterly cold as evidenced by the icicles beneath the first wagon. This East Midlands Division mine, which employed about three hundred men producing in excess of 200,000 tons of saleable coal a year, closed less than two years after this scene was captured. Prior to Nationalisation this mine was owned by Hardwick Colliery Co. Ltd. who had two other collieries in the district, Holmewood, which also had coke ovens and brick works, and Williamthorpe. Those mines were situated just a few miles to the south-west. During NCB days the colliery sat at the southern end of a single-line two mile branch from Bolsover Colliery. *H.A.Gamble.*

Glasshoughton CPD also had some conventional motive power within its precincts and No.3 here, Hawthorn Leslie No.3575 of 1923, is testimony of that. On Saturday 18th April 1970 No.3 is looking to be in fairly good condition even with the coal spillage on its roof. It too is another preserved industrial locomotive and today, in faded blue livery, is resident at Marley Hill shed on the Tanfield Railway. *H.A.Gamble.*

In April 1968, Manvers Main Carbonisation Plant was home to this Fireless 0-6-0 which carried the appropriate name CARBONISATION No.1. Another RSH product, this engine with makers number 7847 of 1955, was very similar to the Glasshoughton engine but without the elevated cab. *H.A.Gamble.*

(centre) Disused at Manvers Main, 16th April 1968, Peckett 0-6-0ST, P1578 of 1921, NCB No.33, was bereft of works plates and carried the legend NOT TO GO. Note the bunker extension which was a later fitting to this compact engine. Whether or not the locomotive worked again is unknown but at about this period the NCB were purchasing new and second-hand diesel locomotives for use at this huge complex. In 1969 P1578 was absent from the Manvers stock but was listed the following year as 'out of use'. *H.A.Gamble.*

(below) Other steam locomotives 'out of use' at Manvers Main in April 1968 included these three 0-6-0ST's. From left they were: No.49 TED, HE3701 of 1950; No.44 WILF, P1891 of 1940; No.11, Yorkshire Engine Co. No.1823 of 1924. Note that this other Peckett has also got a bunker extension. By the end of 1972 Manvers was 'steamless'. *H.A.Gamble.*

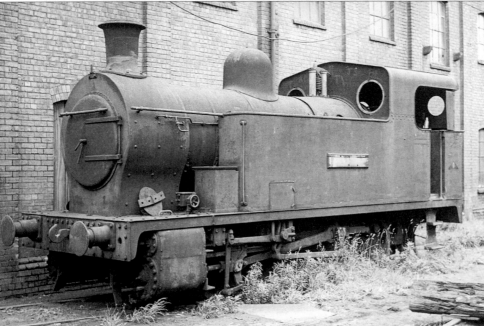

In July 1968 Norwood Coking Plant, Gateshead, employed two diesels and three steam locomotives. The latter comprised a Barclay 0-4-0ST (2317 of 1950), numbered 92, and a pair of RSH 0-4-0 saddletanks, No.72 (7799 of 1954) and No.77 here carrying makers number RSH 7412 of 1948. On Saturday 20th No.77 is resting between turns and looking decidedly unkempt although lining can be seen on the grubby paintwork. The roof especially has suffered from contact with some fixed object a number of times. I must admit that if prototypical liveries and conditions are followed when modelling these industrial locomotives it is possible to use both ends of the spectrum and everywhere between. No.77 is yet another ex NCB locomotive which passed into preservation. *H.A.Gamble.*

You didn't find many 0-8-0 tank engines working in the British coalfields in fact only three are known to have worked colliery lines, all in Lancashire. This 1924 built Nasmyth Wilson product (No.1419), worked at Gin Pit, one of the former Manchester Collieries mines clustered around the western outskirts of that city. Gin Pit was on a two mile circuit of track, with a spur to the Bridgwater Canal at Marsland Green and was connected at both ends to the L&NWR Leigh to Tyldesley line. The circuit of railway was laid down by the Astley & Tyldesley Collieries and originally three other coal mines, St George's, Nook and Bedford were connected to the railway. St George's closed prior to nationalisation whereas Gin merged with Nook in 1955 but that combine closed in 1965 though the washery re-opened in 1966 for a short period, closing for good the following year. Bedford survived to October 1967 with total abandonment of the circuit of railway in April 1968. However, in August 1964 the locomotive workshops and shed attached to Gin Pit were still operational and the 1924 built 0-8-0T which previously carried the name EMANUEL CLEGG had been laid aside in 1958 and was awaiting the scrapman. The 0-8-0T worked the railway here with another similar but earlier, 1910 Nasmyth 0-8-0T named MADEN, withdrawn in 1962. Both had a 12ft wheelbase and 3ft 6in wheels, ideal for the undulating nature of the railway and the tight curvature found in the colliery yards. *H.A.Gamble.*

Hunslet 1557 of 1927, NCB JESSIE laid up at Walkden yard, August 1964 and unlikely to work again. This yellow lined over black liveried tank worked Clewort Hall Collieryl. The railway there was another interesting layout with four mines being served and connections to the Manchester - Wigan lines of both the LYR and L&NWR railways. Redundant since 1961, the 0-4-0T was very much intact, holding on to its name and work plates. *H.A.Gamble.*

Sherburn Hill Colliery in County Durham was the only one of a group of four connected collieries, the others being Littletown, Sherburn and Sherburn House, which became NCB property. Previously owned by Dorman Long & Co. Ltd., the four mines were situated about three miles due east of the city of Durham and encompassed a rectangular area roughly one mile long and half a mile wide, with a colliery situated approximately at each corner. Mining started here in 1835 and eventually all the collieries were rail connected to each other and the BR main line just north of Sherburn station. Coking, gas, household and steam coal were all mined here up to closure in August 1965. In June 1958 one of the colliery locomotives was this dumb-buffered, outside cylinder 0-4-0ST, numbered 148 and carrying the name TAURUS, it was a Hawthorn Leslie product, No.3384 of 1919, and apparently carried no NCB identification. Note in the right background the colliery head frame, both sets of which comprise a combination of rolled steel and lattice girder construction. The screens and washery behind the engine are constructed in the typically 1930's girder frame method with brick in-fill, topped with a corrugated pitched roof. The vast fleet of wagons owned by the National Coal Board included a myriad of types inherited in 1947, and a fixed sided four plank example is just in picture beside the locomotive. Besides the NCB lettering, the legend SHERBURN HILL COLLIERY is stencilled on the lower plank. Sherburn Hill employed over one thousand men and consistently mined over 250,000 tons of saleable coal a year. *R.C.Riley.*

In 1950 the Hunslet Engine Co. supplied eight 0-6-0ST's to the Lancashire coalfield. Cronton Colliery, the most westerly in that county, received this engine and promptly named it CRONTON. Its works number - 3693. The cast nameplates were fixed on the running plate rather than in the more usual position on the tank sides. In this September 1969 photograph the engine was redundant and in a poor external condition, albeit retaining the nameplates. Condemned and scrapped in August 1973, its place was taken by a diesel locomotive. Cronton Colliery, which opened for business in 1922, was amongst the last of the operational mines in Lancashire, closing in 1984. *H.A.Gamble.*

How about this prototype as the subject for a nice industrial locomotive which should be easy enough to model. Regretfully, I can't supply any dimensions to enable a drawing to be made but with a little thought and some trial and error you could get the right result. This 4-wheel battery electric locomotive worked on the Lambton & Hetton Collieries system and was their fleet No.1 It was built by Dick Kerr, No.9537 in 1918 and worked at Philadelphia until withdrawn in 1934. Dick Kerr used to make lots of electric trams for local authorities so perhaps the chassis and wheelbase was similar to one of their tram models. The two sets of buffers obviously allow for shunting both standard and narrow gauge wagons and were a useful fitment to the locomotive. Obviously shunting full wagons in this view, quite where from or to, seems to be mystery - are they the engine sheds from where the train is emerging? It would be entirely possible to make a freelance model of this prototype perhaps using one of the commercially available model tram chassis kits or a powered bogie as motive power. Body and cab construction could be in either sheet brass or plastic card. The oblong nature of the buffer heads should be doddle to fit over trade items. All the other bits, including springs, axlebox covers, couplings, lamps and even works plates are basically available through the trade. Unless you was going to recreate a model of the actual prototype, the livery could be anything you wanted, after all the NCB did not seem too fussy about their locomotive liveries.

Snibston Colliery exchange sidings Thursday 12th May 1983 with two Hunslet 0-6-0 centre-cab diesel hydraulics attending to a train of empty HAA merry-go-round wagons. On its own, at the top of the spur, is NCB No.13, HE 6294 of 1964, whilst the train engine is NCB No.18, HE 6683 of 1967. Based at Desford Colliery, No.18 was one of a number of these type of 0-6-0DH's employed in the area. Sister engine No.16 is now preserved at Snibston Discovery Park. This modern image scene is included to illustrate the ongoing requirement by the NCB for shunting locomotives, even into the 1980's, because not all of the surviving collieries had the true MGR loading system, with the associated bunker or pads, installed. Here we see typical 'wagon load' traffic - necessary for any number of reasons such as colliery output, lack of wagon storage space at the pit, or indifferent permanent way consequently prohibiting access for the much larger BR main line locomotives - being assembled into a train for ongoing delivery to a distant base load power station. However, this scene was soon to become history as Snibston Colliery, one of the oldest in Britain, closed in 1983. Luckily the headframes were preserved and form part of the attraction at the above named park (*see* Snibston Colliery). Desford colliery closed during the following year. *H.A.Gamble.*

Staying with the 'modern image' theme. The location is Chadderton 'B' power station near Oldham. This 236 Megawatt plant, which was commissioned in 1957, was typical of the post-war generating plant built all over the country but now no longer with us - their installed capacity being uneconomical to generate by today's standards. In 1979 one of the plant's 'Industrials' is pushing loaded and well weathered 16-ton mineral wagons into the coal discharge house. The train which brought the coal had probably arrived a couple of days previously to when this view was captured and in the meantime other trainloads will have arrived and empties taken away by BR. The number of wagons required to keep this one small power station supplied with coal was enormous and as for the nation-wide requirements! The

On the same visit to Chadderton 'B', the photographer found this ex BR 204 h.p. 0-6-0 diesel mechanical, formerly of BR Cl.05. it was numbered D2587 dating from 1959. Withdrawn December 1967, it was rebuilt by its original makers and sold to the CEGB, becoming No.1 in the Chadderton fleet. After closure of the power station in the 1980's, the diesel was purchased for preservation. The power station was eventually demolished and the M60 motorway now runs over the site. *Eddie Dixon.*

Coal Fact: The last steel-bodied 16-ton capacity mineral wagon was not delivered to British Railways until 1959.

Shotton Colliery, County Durham, was situated on the north-eastern corner of the town with the same name and connected to the Sunderland-Stockton line at the southern end of the town. On its route from the colliery to the main line, the NCB railway, which was about a mile from end to end, crossed over two public roads as witnessed here in May 1970 with an Andrew Barclay 0-6-0ST crossing the street with a short train. Note there are no gates or barriers and road traffic was protected by a form of traffic light in each direction. Both warning lights, with their zebra like poles, can be seen in this view. So there you have it - industrial railway crossing public road and nothing else except warning lights are required - what could be simpler? Note the BR four-wheel plate wagon behind the locomotive, not the usual mineral wagon and further prove that coal mines required stores like any heavy industrial installation. Shotton Colliery, which also had sixty coke ovens, and a brick works, closed in 1972 and the railway that served it became redundant. During the NCB era the colliery was winding up to 400,000 tons of coal a year with the coke ovens producing 180,000 tons. More than 2,000 of the town's male population were employed by the NCB so it would be taken for granted that the employer's own railway ran across town. *Malcolm Castledine.*

Coal Fact: Of the 110,559,000 tons transported by rail (BR) in 1961, the NCB Divisions despatched the following - East Midlands 31,018,000 tons; North Eastern 22,906,000 tons; South Western 14,894,000 tons; Scottish 12,850,000 tons; Durham 9,913,000 tons; West Midlands 7,397,000; North Western 5,777,000 tons; Northern 4,749,000 tons; South Eastern 1,055,000 tons. Apart from this, another 8,961,000 tons was moved direct from collieries to consumers by private railway, underground or overhead transport system.

Coal Fact: Coal shipments from the West Cumberland ports of Maryport, Whitehaven and Workington in 1947 amounted to 608,485 tons of which Maryport handled 374,902 tons; Whitehaven 220,432 tons and Workington just 13,151 tons. By 1982 Maryport had ceased the shipment of coal, Whitehaven was in mothballs but Workington shipped out 430,322 tons.

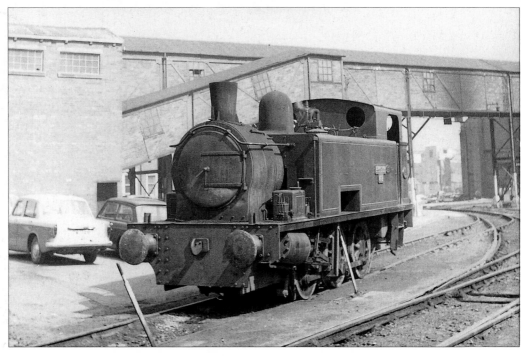

Fryston Colliery, 18th April 1970, with outside cylinder, green liveried, 1955 built Hudswell Clarke 0-6-0T, makers No.1883, carrying the legend Fryston No.2 on a metal plate. *H.A.Gamble.*

Mardy (Maerdy) Colliery in South Wales had two engine sheds, both being simple, modern, brick and concrete structures containing one road each. Although having flat roofs, both sheds had a central louvre type ventilator to allow smoke to exhaust when an engine was inside. Again we have evidence of untidy housekeeping with rubbish strewn around the place. The wheels outside the shed, behind the engine, do not appear to have moved for some time and were probably 'stored' awaiting use on another engine. The outside cylinder saddletank, one time carrying the name MARDY No.2, was a Peckett built engine, No.2151 of 1954 and, in this 10th June 1967 photograph, appears both unidentified and thoroughly neglected. Earmarked for scrap, bits have already been removed to keep MARDY No.1, a similar Peckett 0-6-0ST, operational. *H.A.Gamble.*

Coal Fact: On the eve of Nationalisation of the Coal Industry, there were no less than 125 separate colliery undertakings in Yorkshire. One of the largest firms was Doncaster Amalgamated Collieries Ltd. which had six collieries and employed 16,000 men. In the same county, Amalgamated Denaby Collieries Ltd. operated five collieries with a 9,000 strong workforce.

Maltby Colliery is, in 2005, under private ownership and has been for the past ten years, bringing virtually two million tons of coal to the surface each year. However, in 1967 it was part of the NCB and had undergone a massive modernisation programme both on the surface and below ground. The engine shed was one part of the colliery which did not undergo refurbishment of any kind, even though it dated from the days when the colliery was first operational in 1911. The reason for the lack of investment in 1967 stemmed from the fact that a merry-go-round loading bunker was being erected and the mine would soon have no need for shunting locomotives, steam or diesel. But, the shed is still of interest to us and this 7th October 1967 internal view shows detail not normally given up in photographs. The engine is a Yorkshire Engine Co. 0-6-0ST, No.2485 of 1950, otherwise anonymous and the youngest of three such 0-6-0ST's used at the pit to the end of steam. *H.A.Gamble.*

INDUSTRIAL LOCOMOTIVE FACILITIES

Now, this is a nice gathering around the engine shed at Ackton Hall on Saturday, 17th August 1968. The three engines on view were all operational and from left to right consist: a Bagnall 0-6-0ST with works number 2740 of 1944. It was No.143 in the NCB fleet and had previously been WD No.75152. Next are two Hunslet 0-6-0ST's, AIREDALE No.1440 of 1923, and BEATRICE which also carried the number S119 and was a product of 1945, works No.2705. The last two locomotives passed into preservation at the Embsay and Bolton Abbey Steam Rly, whereas the Bagnall was cut-up. The grounded boiler adds further detail to a tidy scene. The shed roof appears to be a recent addition and consists corrugated asbestos which contrasts nicely with the older weathered brickwork. This Castleford area colliery was winding coal until closure in 1985, annually bringing over half a million tons to the surface. Finally, note the Bedford Dormobile in the right background, wearing the NCB colours (Navy blue) and insignia. For reference, each letter has a full point and a space behind it - N. C. B. *H.A.Gamble.*

In April 1971, the engine shed at Dodworth Colliery appeared to be intact but in need of maintenance. The simple steel framed one road building sat on a dwarf brick wall and was, as can be seen, clad in corrugated asbestos. The doors were timber built and though also still intact were showing signs of misuse. The structure would be an easy model to construct and if you can't quite get those doors hung properly - so what, you are following prototypical practice. *H.A.Gamble.*

The engine sheds found at collieries were as diverse as the headframes and washeries, with no two structures seemingly the same. The running shed at the NCB workshops situated at Walkden, west of Manchester, was one of the more grandiose sheds. Its architecture appears to copy that used for some of the engine sheds of the former Midland or London & North Western railways. Admittedly, to have an engine shed of this size within the mining complex of your layout you would require a fleet of locomotives to justify its existence. The yard was somewhat typical of an industrial setting and even BR did not usually let their locomotive depots become as untidy as this place with the floor ash strewn and only the top surface of the running rails visible. Besides repairing the NCB locomotive fleet in the Lancashire Area, Walkden was also the central workshops for all kinds of colliery machinery repair. The engines on view in this 3rd August 1964 picture, from left to right, outside the shed, were three Hunslet 0-6-0ST's, WARRIOR No.3778 of 1952, REVENGE No.3699 of 1950, WASP No.3808 of 1954. The other engine, out of use beside the shed, is one of the former North Staffordshire 0-6-2T's, built at Stoke in 1921 and purchased by Manchester Collieries when the LMS had no further use for it. This one was named KENNETH and its old LMS number was 2264. *H.A.Gamble.*

The two-road engine shed at Donisthorpe Colliery in Leicestershire was a recent addition by the time of this May 1963 photograph and its simple austere construction of brick, with concrete lintels, and flat roof, should be an easy task over a few evenings. The steel framed windows used in the rear wall are available commercially in model form so the whole building or a representation of such should be an easy enough project for the colliery yard or exchange sidings. The Hawthorn Leslie outside cylinder 0-6-0ST, works No.2611 of 1905, was numbered 2 and carried the name PHOENIX on the same brass plate. Donisthorpe Colliery dated from 1874 and the previous engine shed was probably erected during that period hence the new building. The colliery closed in 1990 after winding over three quarters of a million tons of coal per annum during its peak NCB years. *R.C.Riley.*

Another tidy scene found in Yorkshire on 17th August 1968 was at Water Haigh Colliery where this two road engine shed managed to keep its wooden doors intact. Each of the right-hand doors has a wicket gate, a necessary detail for such large doors. The brickwork is not over ornate and should be easily reproduced by those wanting that to go that little bit farther. Although the roof detail is not apparent, a ventilator can be seen over the left-hand shed; no doubt the other shed also had a least one which was similar. The occupants of the shed are both 0-6-0 tanks; on the left is ELIZABETH, Hudswell Clarke No.1600 of 1927, whilst on the right is WHIT No.4, HC No.1844 of 1951. Water Haigh closed in 1970, its third of a million ton annual contribution to NCB figures finally giving out. *H.A.Gamble.*

Okay, so you've nearly completed the locomotive kit but haven't got round to fitting the wheels or the smokebox door yet. So, instead of leaving the body and frames on the workbench, why not put the assembly on the layout, sited somewhere near to the engine shed and raised slightly above normal centreline as shown here. What you use for packing is up to you but this picture of HE 3171/44 at North Gawber Colliery in April 1971 might give you some ideas. Sunk in the 1850's, North Gawber was one of the longer lived collieries in the North Barnsley area and carried on producing approximately half a million tons of coal a year up to its 1986 closure. The saddletank went the same way as the colliery though much sooner and was scrapped in 1972. *H.A.Gamble.*

Coal Fact: April 1946; The Managing Director of the North Eastern Electric Supply Co. Ltd. said that if all the railways in the country were electrified it would save about 10 million tons of coal per annum.

Coal Fact: October 1946; Manny Shinwell was the principal guest at a dinner to celebrate the raising for the first time of a million tons of coal at Bolsover Colliery.

Coal Fact: August 1954; The Minister of Housing & Local Government informed local authorities in the Forest of Dean that the United Kingdom Atomic Energy Authority would not dispose of waste materials in disused mines in the Forest until the authorities had considered the proposals for dumping atomic waste.

(right) This engine shed at Burradon Colliery, on the Burradon-Backworth system in Northumberland, was one of two at the site, the other being a much more modern building. This one-road through structure was, as can be seen, built of brick with a pitched roof clad in corrugated iron. The original arch, if indeed it was ever used as such, has been in-filled with bricks laid on a simple rolled steel joist. The doors at this end, which were probably never closed are, in this June 1969 photograph, in surprisingly good condition although perhaps are requiring a couple of coats of paint. The side walls of this shed had arched windows although the gloom inside tells us that glass cleaning was not a priority here. A brick built lean-to, complete with its own doorway and chimneyed stove, graces the south wall. Study of the well weathered brickwork reveals a shed which is obviously quite old but is still functioning as a shelter for the various locomotives working the colliery. Ashes, clinker and other debris are strewn around the immediate area whilst a nice pile is building up alongside a relatively young Hudswell 0-6-0T No.1823 of 1949, NCB Northumberland 1&2 Area, number 38. *Malcolm Castledine.*

(bottom) Prior to nationalisation, some of the larger coal mining concerns could boast railway systems which were not only very big but also self contained in every way. The Lambton & Hetton system in County Durham was one such undertaking and at its main railway centre at Philadelphia it had workshops and engine sheds to rival many of the constituent companies borne into the railway Grouping in 1923. The distinctive cab profile of its locomotives was one of the memorable aspects of the Lambton system but its method of coaling locomotives was probably unique in the United Kingdom. The elevated track carried wagons high above the shed yard enabling the bottom discharge wagons to drop their contents onto chutes which were positioned over the locomotive bunker. Very similar to the coaling stages found at many BR sheds up to the end of steam but not as labour intensive - a one man operation in principle and not much different from the staiths found on the river banks in the north-east. This structure is built on a steel girder (RSJ) frame topped by timber planking and running rails. Note the curve running to the ramp out of picture on the left of the frame. The date is 12th June 1965 and the 0-6-2T is No.53 one of the ex Taff Vale Railway engines working here. On the right is No.31, one of the Kitson built stud. *H.A.Gamble.*

Coal Fact: Only a fraction the size of its southern counterpart, the North Wales coalfield was nevertheless an important source of high volatile caking coal from the mid-1800s. By 1870 it was producing just over 2 million tons per annum rising to 3 million tons by the turn of the century. Its output in the record year of 1913 was 3.5 million tons and, sharing the fortunes of the rest of the UK mining industry, its output by 1945 was down to just over 2 million tons. After nationalisation the inevitable closures occurred and in 1974 only two collieries remained working - Point of Ayr, on the Flintshire coast and Bersham in Denbighshire with the latter closing within a couple of years. Point of Ayr closed in 1996.

Coal Fact: The main line railway wagons which the NCB inherited were rented to the Ministry of Fuel & Power before they passed to the British Transport Commission in 1948.

When Keith Pirt visited Williamthorpe Colliery in April 1967 he had somewhat better weather to contend with than Malcolm Castledine. These two views of the locomotive servicing facility show the two 'on loan' 0-6-0T's having a quiet moment. Fires will have been tended, water tanks topped up and no doubt the bunkers will have been replenished with coal, however that was delivered. Both crews will be either on a rest break or will have ended their shift. The scene is pleasing to the modeller in many ways: The water tank with its brick plinth columns is easy to model. No engine shed is required, at least not in these pictures although the crews seem to be catered for. Do you like your yard tidy or otherwise? If the latter then all the ingredients are on show here. *both pictures - Keith Pirt.*

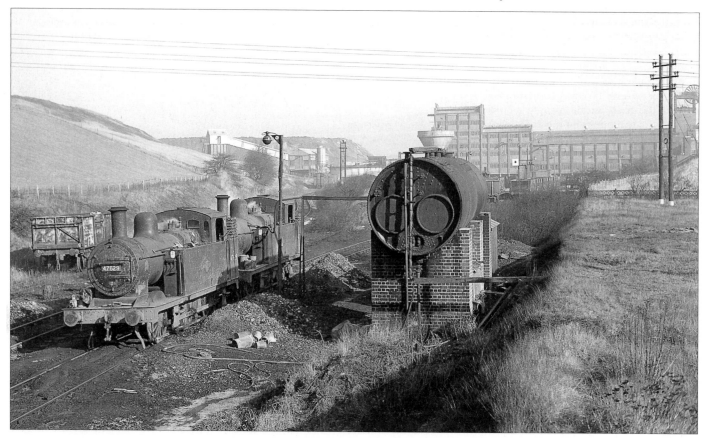

The Austerity 0-6-0ST could be found at NCB sites all over the country from Kent to Glamorgan, Leicester to Lancashire, Nottinghamshire to Northumberland - basically every coalfield had them and in most cases dozens of them. This example was working at the Backworth complex in July 1967 and is seen on the engine shed yard at Eccles Colliery and is being got ready for its day's labour. The NCB did not seem to have a standard livery for their locomotive fleet and colours varied between blue, green, red, black, yellow and other indescribable shades. The same went for the lining and that varied from the exquisite multiple lining to the non-existent. Backworth No.4 was somewhere in between with a very subtle single line and looked about right. The driver bending over and inspecting the motion adds another nice touch for the static model and it puts the size of these large tank engines into perspective. In the background a discarded Lancashire boiler gets a second life as a water tank for the shed, note the two substantial brick piers supporting it. *Malcolm Castledine.*

The shed housing the NCB engine at Bardon Mill Colliery in Northumberland was of an austere appearance being of lightweight construction with a steel frame, infilled with rendered brick screens which had a thickness of just one course. The simple pitched roof was of corrugated iron which in this May 1970 view was showing its twenty-odd year age. Note the dirty window panes and of course the broken and absent glass. Adding that kind of detail to a finished model gives it that little bit more authenticity. The colliery here was developed during the late 1940's and contributed between one and two hundred thousand tons of coal each year to the NCB total until closure in 1973. The outside cylinder 0-4-0ST, NCB No.40, an Andrew Barclay product, No.2280 of 1950, was not the usual locomotive employed here and was standing in for a much older Hawthorn Leslie 0-4-0ST dating from 1906. Just beyond the extremely rusty, though operational, 21-ton BR coal hoppers was the Newcastle to Carlisle main line. *Malcolm Castledine.*

Williamthorpe Colliery departure sidings in June 1955 with loaded wagons being marshalled into trains. The aspect is north-east, with the colliery behind the camera, the former GCR main line runs north from right to left and at this point the Chesterfield Loop diverged north-westwards, although not apparent from this angle. The colliery branch laid down by the GCR can be seen running along the edge of the raised ground on which this group of sidings are founded. Access to and from the GC was via the underbridge on the right, the other bridge in view spanned the A617 road. One particular point which struck me about the wagons was the low number of 'bog standard', steel bodied 16-ton mineral wagons which, by 1955 at least, should have been in the majority. However, the wooden bodied wagons from the pre-nationalised period dominate although most have long lost their previous identity. The yard is strewn with large and small coal, with little hillocks between the running rails, the rails themselves are visible as shiny lines amongst the spillage. This should be easy enough to recreate and you do not have to paint the sides of the rails that rusty colour associated with the main lines and such like - matt black or similar would do instead. The sidings have been brought into modern times with a lighting tower which is well secured - I wonder how many shunters tripped over those stays when the tower was first installed? *British Railways.*

Lynemouth Colliery was one of the larger NCB production units and in this June 1969 view of its departure sidings we get a good idea of the size of a large multi siding complex. It was usual for two locomotives to be employed round-the-clock here and one of them, NCB No.42 a RSH outside cylinder 0-6-0ST No.7768 of 1954, is making its way towards the screens, towing a coal tender. The loaded wagons, note the preference for hoppers in the North Eastern Region, are 21 and 24 ton types in various condition but with a fairly uniform load which, from a side view, would barely be visible. This 'small' coal was probably bound for a power station or large industrial concern. *Malcolm Castledine.*

WAGONS, WAGONS, WAGONS & Other Vehicles

An undated photograph of Ashton Moss Colliery wagon No.5, which appears to be newly constructed or at least nicely repainted, 16-tonner. Although slightly blurred, it is just possible to make out the legend *When empty return to Crowthorne Junction L.N.W.R.*, which basically dates it before Grouping, however, the wagon could probably have carried that particular legend for many years after 1923. *Salford Mining Museum.*

Coal Fact: January 1950; Mr. R.Woodward, the oldest miner at Hylton Colliery, retired after 63 years in the mines. He was 75 years old and started work at the age of 12 years for 10½d. (4.2p) a day.

Coal Fact: Whilst the number of brick works owned by the NCB was reduced from 85 in 1947 to 75 by 1951, the output of bricks increased from 389 million to 473 million. Of these, approximately 25% were used by the NCB whilst the large balance were sold outside the industry. In 1956 the production of 522 million bricks saw the amount equal some 12% of the national total. Declining sales and market trends brought the brick making business profits tumbling down and in 1973 the nineteen remaining NCB owned plants, which were still in profit to the tune of £1 million p.a., were sold off for £5,600,000.

This circa 1920 photograph is included to show off a nicely weathered 12-ton, 5-plank, end door coal wagon at New Moss Colliery, near Ashton-under-Lyne, complete with twenty-nine members of the mine workforce. Numbered 505, the wagon appears to be full of boiler coal and is trimmed off ready for its journey to the customer. I'm not sure just when this colliery closed but was not vested into the NCB, at least not under that name. It also does not appear in the LMS *List of Collieries* dated July 1937, so it may well have ceased operations shortly after the Grouping of the railways. The picture is also a slice of social history of the period with not only most of the men wearing waistcoats but all of them are sporting the same type of head wear. Finally, note the sleeper spacing of the yard track. *Salford Mining Museum.*

Virtually every colliery, many coal merchants, coal factors and municipal utilities had their own fleets of coal wagons. Cardiff based Cwmaman Coal Co. had a large fleet and in 1926 the standard company livery name included the large letter 'C'. Besides the horizontal display of the name, there was also the curved version as can be seen on the seventh vehicle along this line of empty wagons outside the former Taff Vale Railway engine shed at Cardiff Cathay's in April 1926. Behind the front row is a line of Cody Brothers wagons, again empty and awaiting onward transit back to the respective 'pits'. Note that some 'empty' wagons have been usefully utilised to carry imported pit props from the docks back to the colliery, a normal everyday occurrence. *Authors collection.*

J27 No.1027 heads north-east out of Newcastle Central station towards one of the Northumberland washeries with a train of former North Eastern Railway 20-ton hopper wagons in 1935. These impressive vehicles were built to satisfy a need to transport lots of coal in as short a train as possible, through an area where coal trains virtually monopolised the running lines of the railways. A train of these hopper wagons would constitute about two-thirds the length of train made up of ordinary mineral and open wagons carrying the same amount of coal. *E.V.Fry collection.*

The ubiquitous (on the North Eastern Railway anyway) NER 20-ton hopper wagon used for coal service. This example was, as can be seen, braked on one side only (the unseen side here), whilst on the visible side are the levers, rods, fulcrums and connections for working the bottom discharge mechanism beneath the wagon. This wagon was numbered 2096 in the fleet and similar wagons carried Nos.7814, 10927, 11142, etc.

Coal Fact: 1886 - Coal owners in Durham forced the North Eastern Railway to give them a direct route (Dunston Extension) to the River Tyne for their minerals. Previously the NER 'bottlenecked' all production through Tyne Dock and delays ensued.

Virtually every wagon in this coal train has the legend LOCO fixed to the sides in raised metal letters. The location is Smithy Bridge water troughs near Rochdale and the Widnes based Stanier 8F heading this westbound coal train in August 1950, is No.48772. I have no idea which company decorated their locomotive coal wagons in this style, although the Lancashire & Yorkshire certainly didn't, but there were a number of varying themes in the LMS constituents alone and, I have a feeling that these are such wagons. Anyway, here again is further proof that some coal trains were exclusive to a particular traffic. *Jim Davenport.*

(*below*) At the other end of the wagon size scale is this train of mainly four and five plank wagons in coal service in June 1929. Composed of various LNER and LMS varieties, the well loaded train is at Eastfield being hauled by J37 No.9457. Basically, your coal trains can be made up from any type of open or mineral wagon that you have available. When loaded even these short bodied wagons look impressive when put together. *E.V.Fry collection.*

At first glance, there is nothing remarkable about this picture of WD No.90143 surrounded by loaded coal wagons at Rose Grove circa January 1963. It has been snowing, it was cold and the coal was probably frozen solid in the wagons. However, a look at the wooden bodied wagon immediately behind the WD's tender will reveal the legend 'COND' announcing that the wagon was in fact condemned and should not have been in service, never mind loaded. It may have been on its way for breaking up at some works or rail connected private yard but it certainly would not be en route to such a place with about ten tons of coal inside. The truth probably lies with the weather. The winter of 1962/63 was one of the harshest of the 20th Century and coal was of course in great demand, as it is at such times. Not only power stations require more than usual but also gas works (before the flood of natural gas from the North Sea), industry, and coal merchants, the latter could not get enough of it and if the coal was stuck inside a wagon it was of little use to anyone, nor was the wagon. So, as an emergency measure, condemned wagons which were not too clapped out saw a new lease of life albeit short, helping the country to keep warm once again.

The first two vehicles of this train being drawn at Cadley Hill Colliery by RSH 0-6-0ST PROGRESS, consist of two former BR steel open wagons which had recently joined the NCB fleet. Both have been quickly lettered (CG presumably means Church Gresley) and numbered, CG 17 the more so it seems with its tare weight and the legend 'landsale' looking like the work of unskilled graffiti 'artists'. CG 16's paint job does not appear to be so crudely applied. So, if your painting/signwriting skills are not too good there is no need to worry - just show your friends this picture when they criticise your handiwork. The date was 16th July 1970. *H.A.Gamble.*

The NCB Internal User wagon fleet was not only vast, it was also extremely varied. The modern steel bodied 21-ton hoppers found in Durham and Northumberland, for instance, covered a number of different designs. This rather smart example was in use at Derwenthaugh coking plant in 1969 and was numbered 6937. Its side supports consisted box section steel, welded to the body and extending right down to the wagon solebar. Note the abbreviated plant name D-HAUGH which was a size smaller than the NCB legend. Nos.6683 and 6970 were other examples at this plant. Similar wagons, such as No.6697, carried the plant name in full over two panels. A Backworth based wagon was No.91D1781, whilst Whittle Colliery had a number of wagons which all had the prefix 9300 with a back slash. Other similar Backworth wagons were 91D 1791. *Malcolm Castledine.*

Another modern 21-ton hopper was No.6653 which was of a similar profile to No.6937 but used riveted angle iron for the side supports. These supports, it will be noted, followed the line of the hopper side and did not project vertically to the solebar. Other examples of this design were numbered 6401, 6576 and 6595. *Malcolm Castledine.*

The Bowes system also had a large number of Internal User wagons such as this 14-ton steel bodied hopper numbered 6300. The NCB legend on this one contains full points whilst the lettering of the BOWES legend is about half the size. Other wagons of this type were Nos.6308, 7004, 7008 and 7062. *Malcolm Castledine.*

Besides the steel bodied hoppers employed at Bowes, a number of older straight sided wooden bodied hopper wagons were still at work in the late 1960's. The sloping ends of the hopper are not discernible from the outside of the vehicle unless it is empty so, with a load it appears just like any other six-plank wagon and can be easily converted from such. This 10-ton example, No.1149, incorporates a metal inspection ladder just over the buffer shank. Other 1960's survivors from this once large Bowes fleet include Nos.297, 412, 477, 684 and 1207; an eight plank version was No.1509. *Malcolm Castledine.*

Coal Fact: Up to the implementation of the Merry-Go-Round scheme, the Electricity generators and the NCB were guilty of using BR's wagons for the storage of coal, hoarding them by the thousand throughout the country. BR were well aware of this problem and had worked out that an average mineral wagon in their fleet worked about 21,000 ton-miles per annum - not very productive at all. By 1962, it was realised that the new high capacity mineral wagons which were then being developed and were to be introduced for the MGR scheme could work as much as 1,458,000 ton-miles per annum - an improvement of nearly seven thousand percent (7000%)! It was envisaged that a fleet of just over 10,000 high capacity mineral wagons could do the job of the 150,000 mineral wagons of varying capacities then employed for the power station coal traffic.

NCB wagon No.91A/344 was a 21-ton hopper which incorporated box section steel supports to the vertical steel side sheets with fillets continuing the line and supporting the angled sides. This wagon was in use at Mill Colliery. Similar vehicles at Derwenthaugh were numbered 6665 and 6691, whilst a Backworth based wagon was numbered 91A/348. Note the off-centre NCB insignia and 'Internal Use Only' legend. Even the load appears uneven. *Malcolm Castledine.*

This NCB wooden bodied hopper wagon, SRW10692, was in use in Northumberland and as can be seen from the legend on the side was working at the Ashington group of collieries. This view was taken at Fenwick Colliery in 1967. The distinctive sloping sides had two main vertical straps which in some cases consisted bolted or riveted steel strips, or thin wooden supports faced with a steel strap. Two 15in x 6in steel rubbing plates were fixed to each side, midway up the body. Similar vehicles with the same SRW prefix were numbered: 96, 10114, 10404, 10708 and 10723. *Malcolm Castledine.*

Whenever wagons misbehaved on the NCB's own internal railway systems, the offenders often ended up 'grounded' never to work again, and were left where they lay to rot or be collected by a scrap merchant. Sometimes the wagons were damaged after collision or derailment and were deemed beyond repair. These two miscreants at Bates Colliery in Northumberland, have been discarded with damage. Although not the subject of the original photograph, the grounded wagons give us enough prototypical detail for possible use on our own layouts. Nearest is a steel bodied NCB version of the BR 16-ton mineral wagon, possibly at this late date, June 1969, it was an exBR wagon purchased by the NCB for their Internal fleet. It appears to have had a few patches welded onto its sides but in this view it seems to be heavily damaged. Behind is wooden bodied open with a definite twist to its bodywork. Within the trains on view, there are a number of ordinary steel bodied 16-ton mineral wagons which may well have been former BR vehicles. It would be easy enough to transfer some of your own BR fleet to an NCB fleet simply by painting them black and applying suitable transfers, some of the red oxide versions were just lettered if the paintwork was in good condition and I should imagine that some of the grey liveried wagons kept that colouring when they changed owners. Note the NCB lettering is of varying sizes and some wagons even have full points after each letter. One thing the lettering has in common - it is all sans serif. Known numbers for these wagons include: 9252/1347; 9252/1697. *Malcolm Castledine.*

The 'Jubilee' wagon. Built in their hundreds for colliery use, I'm not sure if there is a commercial model equivalent of this NCB Internal User side tipping spoil wagon. This example was photographed at Measham Colliery in Leicestershire but they were found at mines all over the country. Although the body work might present a challenge for the scratch builder, the wheels look to be a tad more difficult to recreate. The date of the photograph is 16th October 1965, some twenty-one years before the colliery closed so this wagon probably saw a lot more work before retirement. *H.A.Gamble.*

> **Coal Fact:** July 1950; the first lorry which actually bagged coal on the rounds was used in Lincolnshire.

(*opposite*) Besides redundant wagons and brake vans, the main line railway companies also supplied old coaching stock to the mine owners. The Ashington Group of collieries in Northumberland, though not unique in running passenger trains for their miners, were certainly one of the largest users of former mainline passenger stock. Up until the 1970's trains were run around the system which encompassed a virtual circuit from Ashington to Ellington, Lynemouth, Woodhorn and others. At Ashington in June 1966 this three coach rake had two former North Eastern Railway toplights in its make-up. Twenty years into NCB ownership, the carriages are appropriately lettered. *H.A.Gamble.*

This former Midland Railway 6-wheel brakevan was in use at Florence Colliery in March 1968. Although it appears to have no NCB identification, it is still in reasonable condition considering it must have been at least sixty-six years old by then. Why the colliery used the brake is unknown to the author, however, the mine was situated on the edge of Longton but was connected to the former North Staffordshire main line between Stoke and Stone. The distance between the pit and the main line interchange at Trentham, amounted to nearly two miles by rail over what might be described as undulating topography, especially for loaded trains. Perhaps somebody might let me know. Florence was winding coal until 1992 so somebody must know the full story. *H.A.Gamble.*

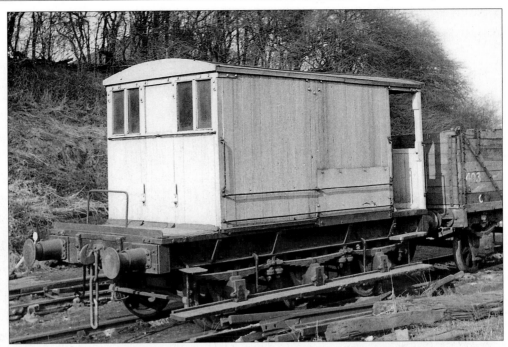

Also at Ashington on 11th June 1966 was this former Furness Railway passenger coach with its NCB lettering more tightly spaced and with full points. Just below the windows the legend BATES MEN ONLY is discernible, however, its presence at Ashington is unclear as Bates 'Pit' is some distance away at South Blyth and to get the carriage here must have entailed at trip over BR trackage! I believe a brown livery was applied to these passenger vehicles though some were also in black, whatever it was, you would have been hard pressed to see through all the accumulated grime. *H.A.Gamble.*

Coal Fact: February 1950; Shipley No.2 opencast site at Shipley Hall, Derbyshire, won its millionth ton of coal.

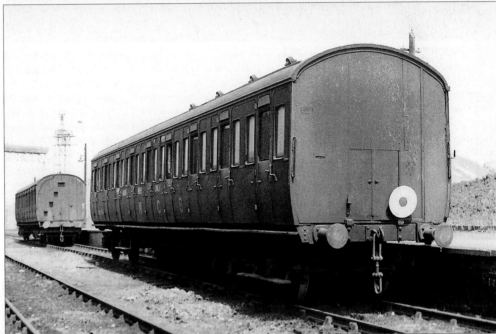

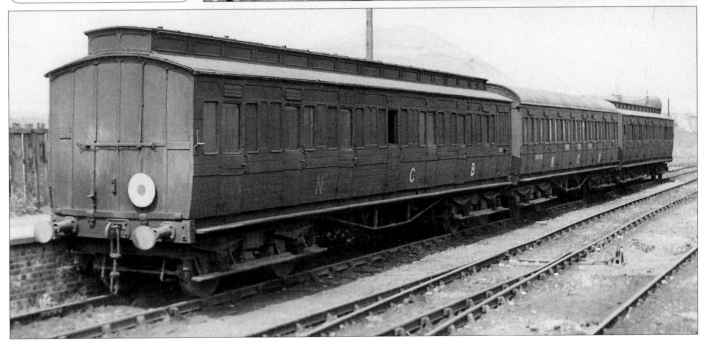

(above & left) BR 21 ton hopper wagons of mixed design. Another mix is the coal loads which vary from very small industrial types to large household coals. *(below)* The Hornby (ex-Dapol) 4mm version as modified and detailed by Dave Bradwell using his Detailing Etch and Modelmaster transfers *(bottom photograph by Dave Bradwell, the other two by Malcolm Castledine).*

Coal Fact: July 1947 - Dr. J. H. Jones, Divisional Chief Scientist to the Northern Area, NCB, stated that coal reserves in Durham and Northumberland amounted to 5,000 million tons, enough to last 100 years.

ASTLEY GREEN COLLIERY

Just to the west of Manchester, on the south side of the East Lancashire Road (A580), at Astley, there stands a coal mine headframe which dominates the flat landscape surrounding it. The headframe is a surviving piece of industrial archaeology marking the site of one of Lancashire's most productive collieries - Astley Green. Today the colliery site, aptly named Astley Green Colliery Museum, is owned by the local authority but is looked after by the Red Rose Steam Society Ltd. The RRSS is a registered charity and the volunteer members, with former miners amongst their number, maintain the buildings, machinery and artefacts associated with the now long disappeared industry of coal mining in Lancashire.

The surviving headframe, which in 2012 will celebrate it's centenary, is unique in that it is the only one of its type left in northern England - a lattice girder headframe. The preservation of the frame is a priority if it is not to be lost forever because the elements have taken their toll over the thirty-five years since the mine closed. However, the frame is still in a condition where remedial maintenance could preserve it for another hundred years or more, making it a fitting monument to one of the county's largest and most important lost industries.

One part of the colliery which has been preserved to its former glory is the No.1 winding engine, a massive piece of machinery which has to be seen to be believed. Inside its own building, the engine and associated winding drum have undergone a dramatic restoration which allows visitors to look at one of the most powerful winding engines ever built in this country. Next is the creation of a boiler house.

The Red Rose Steam Society were good enough to allow me access to their photographic collection and the following illustrations are taken from that collection. Without the kindness and enthusiasm of the members of the RRSS, a great part of this volume could not have been produced as it is here. The views are intended to show the development of the colliery from the earliest days, through the years of modernisation and finally the closure and demolition of much of the infrastructure. Most of the aspects will hopefully give modellers further information and the inspiration to create a model colliery, or at least a section of one, on their model railway layout.

Whenever you are in south Lancashire why not make a visit to the Astley Green Colliery Museum. You will get a chance to look over the old and discarded machinery awaiting restoration, perhaps have a conducted tour of the engine house given by one of the friendly RRSS members, or walk around the displays which give an insight as to what life was really like working underground. On most Sunday's you can get a trip around the site and over to the canal aboard the narrow gauge man riding cars, hauled over the specially laid track by diesel locomotives which previously worked underground at Calverton Colliery in Nottinghamshire.

Finally, I would like to thank the Red Rose Steam Society and its membership, particularly Bob Bruce, Richard Walls, and Roy Sheffield. All of whom made me very welcome on my first unannounced visit to the museum and have since given their time and attention during subsequent visits.

An aerial view of Astley Green Colliery in 1963 looking due south. A good idea of the size of the mine, not including the outlying tips, car park and housing, can be realised by the number of wagons in the stationery trains at bottom left. The headframe on the right of the complex is No.1 (downcast) whilst the slightly smaller No.2 (upcast) is on the left. Note also that the winding houses are scaled according with No.1 being larger than its counterpart. Between them is the old boiler house which had no less than sixteen Lancashire type boilers installed. Note that the two tall brick chimneys are now redundant as all the mine's electrical power is generated at the modern powerhouse which is the tall lighter coloured building on the left, with the smoking chimney. On the south side of the site are the original screens with the larger NCB-built structure attached. Quite a number of wagons can be seen in the sidings serving the screens. Beyond the screens is the Bridgwater canal with a couple of barges evident near the road overbridge. Even at this late date ongoing new construction is evident in a bid to make the colliery more efficient. As a prototype for modelling this mine would take up a lot of space, not to mention time, but this view shows how a large Lancashire colliery was laid out on fairly flat and level terrain.

This is the scene at Astley Green just prior to 1912 when the two shafts were still being sunk and prior to the erection of the first steel headframe. Just digging the shafts, in this case each over 2,500 ft deep, required elaborate surface buildings and lots of cash reserves. However, prior to WW1 Britain was the largest coal producer in the world and had every intention of remaining so. Therefore, such development as seen here, which often took many years to complete before coal was being wound at economic rates, was seen by all as quite normal. The Pilkington Coal Co. Ltd., were responsible for sinking this pit which started in 1908 and it was not until about 1914 when the first saleable coal was wound.

(opposite) Sat on top of its massive brick built bank, the lattice steelwork of the No.1 headframe starts to take shape around the timber built framework of the sinking/development headgear. Head-Wrightson were the makers of the new headframe and contractors for its erection. Their men appear to show a total disregard to the dangers of working at such heights but being experienced, full of bravado anyway and not having a H&SE to bother them, they got on with the job after this interlude for a photographic portrait. Note that the headgear in this view has a number of temporary components within its frame when compared with the picture showing the completed headframe. In the background the No.2 (upcast) shaft headframe is still busy winding men, materials, spoil and sometimes coal whilst the mine is being developed half a mile below Lancashire.

Surviving mine tubs at Astley Green 2005. In 1947 the mining industry employed seventy-seven different wheels diameter for these pit tubs but later 'standardised' with sixteen.

Want to know what to do with any redundant mine tubs on your layout - ground them, add a few pipes and use them as water or oil tanks as here. Don't forget to leave the wheels on, its much more authentic.

The No.1 (downcast) shaft headgear at Astley Green, seen from the bank, shortly after completion in 1912. Note that the temporary tie-rods, bracing and securing the main legs of the frame during construction, have now been replaced by small, box profile lattice girders. To the right is the No.1 chimney and behind that the winding house. Note the shaped holes in the end wall for the 2,600+ long winding rope. A normal square hole would have been too big if the rope was to be allowed to travel across the winding drum as it rotated, so this particular profile was built into the brickwork.

No.1 shaft headframe virtually complete but still harbouring the wooden development frame within its structure. Note the size of the newly built winding engine house compared with the original building dwarfed before it. The presence of side tipping wagons reveal that the pit bank is still being created

The first locomotive to work at Astley Green Colliery was this outside cylinder 0-4-0 saddletank, appropriately named ASTLEY, seen here beside the boiler house in August 1908 just after delivery from makers Peckett (1164/08). This engine worked the yards until 1935 when records of it cease.

This circa 1912 view of No.2 shaft headgear during the sinking phase, gives us plenty to dwell on regarding using this as a prototype to model for a small mine. Virtually everything is here, even a spoil chute which with a bit more elaboration could become a coal chute. The scale of the whole scene could easily be created in a small space. Note the Lancashire boilers waiting to be installed.

The new screens under construction circa 1919. The concrete foundations for all this steelwork had been laid in 1915 but building was delayed no doubt due to wartime shortages. The sidings serving the screens numbered nineteen when the work was completed. This skeletal view gives a good idea of what the 'steelwork' of your screens should look like prior to cladding the outer walls.

The No.1 winding engine house. This building, with its huge winding engine, is still extant and is well worth a visit. Admitted, the prototype structure is large but can be easily scaled down just by taking a third or more off the all round dimensions. Instead of being seven windows long as here, knock it down to four and have just two instead of three in the end walls. As an aside, just look at that ladder.

The pit bank tipplers on the south side of No.1 shaft with mine cars about to be tipped at some time in the early 1960's. The winding cages at Astley Green had three decks with two cars on each level but before the mine closed the cages were replaced by hoppers which had a greater capacity. From a modelling standpoint, the enclosed tipplers would require less work to recreate than the open type where lots of niggardly detail is exposed.

(*above*) The roadway between the two headframes and below the pit bank, with No.2 (upcast) shaft dominating the scene. Firstly, note that No.2 headframe is of different construction to No.1. Here H and I section girders have been employed giving a somewhat lightweight appearance compared with No.1. Also, look how the shaft is virtually enclosed, not only within the two-storey pithead building built around it but also inside the frame. Modelling a headframe in this style would cut down on the amount of structural styrene needed but a building of sorts would have to be constructed for a base. The roadway caters not only for motor vehicles but also two gauges of railway track. Note how pipelines are kept clear of traffic by the use of steel supporting legs.

(*left*) East side detail of No.2 at closure, 7th July 1970. This pit was known as the Worsley mine.

(*opposite, top*) A view of the reception building where the mine cars came together on the upper level and left on the lower level after discharge. The two separate levels of mechanical 'creeper' ramps are well advanced in this circa 1919 photograph.

(*opposite*) The completed screens in 1920 shortly after commissioning. Note the brick clad walls and the eastlight roof over the lower section of the building. The creeper ramps have two continuous 'conveyors' installed between the tracks and each loaded mine car was grabbed by two hooks at the bottom and propelled up the ramp and given enough momentum to carry on its journey into the shed unaided. These screens do not have coal washing facilities, the coal was simply graded prior to loading into the standard gauge wagons. Note the lack of windows in the walls, all natural illumination was gained through the part glazed roof of this shed. A later, NCB period, extension which included a washery was built on this face of the screens. Further extensions and alterations made the original building virtually unrecognisable.

Astley Green engine shed in October 1967 with ALLEN built in 1944 by Hudswell Clark No.1777, EDWARD built by Hawthorn Leslie in 1916 No.3184, and JAMES another 1944 built engine but by Robert Stephenson & Hawthorn their No.7175, outside. None of this trio reached preservation and were all cut up in 1968.

Steam locomotives associated with Astley Green Colliery:-

Maker/Wks No.	Type	Name/No.	Years	Disposal.
AB 1704/20	0-4-0ST oc.	CARBON	19??-1962	to Bank Hall, c/u 1968.
HC 1776/44	0-6-0ST ic.	HARRY 71499	1945-1970	pres. Shropshire Loco Soc.
HC 1777/44	0-6-0ST ic.	ALLEN	195?-1968	from Ellesmere c/u 1968.
HC 1812/48	0-4-0ST oc.	CARR	1948-196?	to William, c/u 1972.
HE 1475/25	0-6-0T ic.	BRIDGWATER	1925-1968	c/u 1968.
HR 3302/45	0-6-0ST ic.	STANLEY	195?-196?	exEllesmere, to Ladysmith, c/u 1975.
HE 3696/50	0-6-0ST ic.	RESPITE	1950-196?	to Ellesmere, preserved.
HE 3697/50	0-6-0ST ic.	RENOWN	195?-1968	exGin Pit, c/u 1968.
HE 3698/50	0-6-0ST ic.	REPULSE	1950-1970	pres. Lakeside & Haverthwaite Rly.
HE 3699/50	0-6-0ST ic.	REVENGE	1950-1970	c/u 1976.
HE 3778/52	0-6-0ST ic.	WARSPITE	196?-196?	exEllesmere, to Brackley, c/u 1976.
HE 3823/54	0-6-0ST ic.	WARRIOR	1954-1960	to Ellesmere, preserved.
HE 3842/56	0-6-0ST ic.	WITCH	1956-1968	c/u 1968.
HE 3844/57	0-6-0ST ic.	WEASEL	1959-196?	exGin Pit, to Haig, c/u 1976.
HL 3184/16	0-6-0ST oc.	EDWARD	1916-1968	c/u 1968.
KS 3068/17	0-6-0T oc.	FRANCIS	1919-1968	c/u 1968.
MW XX/65	0-6-0T ic.	BEDFORD	19??-1947	c/u 1950.
P 1164/08	0-4-0ST oc.	ASTLEY	1908-c1935	—
RSH 7174/44	0-6-0ST ic.	71520	195?-196?	exGin Pit, to Ellesmere, c/u 1968.
RSH 7175/44	0-6-0ST ic.	JAMES 71521	1947-48, 64-67	c/u 1968.
RSH 7293/45	0-6-0ST ic.	HUMPHREY	1945-1970	to Parsonage c/u 1976.
SS 2742/78	0-4-0ST oc.	BLACK DIAMOND	19??-1949	c/u 1950.

Coal Fact: In Great Britain during 1938 some 912 coal mines employed 32,059 horses underground and of these 991 were killed and 3,821 injured in accidents. By 1962 the numbers equated to 6,471 horses employed underground in 322 coal mines and of which 148 were killed with another 789 were injured in accidents.

(opposite) Just upstream/eastwards from Astley Green was another canalside loading bank known as Boothsbank Tippler. Of steel construction with timber cladding, this would make a nice model for those of you who have room for a canal or associated basin on your layout.

(above) Downstream/west of Astley Green, at Marsland Green, this tippler loaded barges on the Bridgwater with coal from either Bedford, Gin Pit or Nook collieries. Both wide and narrow barges were catered for and during a 24 hour period as many as forty boats could be loaded. This 1930's scene shows a narrow boat with accommodation for the bargee, albeit small, awash with dust. These narrow boats could easily load eighty tons or so of small coal which in most cases was en route to a public utility.

(right) Astley Green Colliery supplied coal by barge to Westwood power station in Wigan and, in the easterly direction, to Barton power station. To load the barges with the boxes of coal, this vertical boilered travelling steam crane was employed. The boats/barges were essentially narrow boats and had neither accommodation nor motive power and relied on a separate barge to tow them.

Besides the railway access to its premises, every mine needs a pedestrian and motor vehicle entrance. These are the main gates at Astley Green in 1970 shortly after the colliery closed. Such gates are available in 4mm scale, and probably other scales too, so why not add a nice finishing touch such as these. The pillars can be easily fabricated in plastic card. Don't forget the flower boxes on the office window sills.

The railway yard at Astley Green after closure, looking eastward toward Boothstown. With most of the tracks still in situ, it is possible to see the course of many of them. Coming in from the middle right is the line which crossed the canal to gain access to the yard known as Astley Green sidings where loaded trains were made up prior to onward transit to customers via the main line railways. Opened in 1912, the connection consisted a one and half mile long branch line built across the Bridgwater Canal and then Astley Moss, in a north-south direction, to the former London & North Western Railway's main line between Manchester and Liverpool (the original 1830 L&MR), just east of Astley station. Sidings were laid near to the main line. The junction allowed direct connection from the yard to either the east (Up) or westbound (Down) lines but incoming empty trains had to reverse off the main line into the yard. Note the inclined conveyor spanning the canal, this took spoil from the now demolished washery to a bunker on the opposite bank where road vehicles tipped the dirt on a vast tip. When the colliery closed, spoil from the tip was used to in-fill the two deep shafts.

The headframe in close-up -

The diagonal support legs of the headframe have brick foundations but concrete was often substituted. Rivets secured the legs to base plates.

Viewed from the opposite side, the brick base is showing signs of weathering, as is the steelwork of the leg.

One of the support leg foundations enclosed in a concrete jacket. The brick bund wall was added after the colliery closed as the original ground level was raised inadvertently during the general demolition and tipping of spoil.

From the other side, the connection between the support leg and one of the diagonal supports is just evident. These supports were in turn fixed to a large concrete block hidden beneath the surface.

Support for the six main legs (three on each side) was given by the massive brick foundation ring atop the shaft.

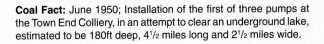

Coal Fact: June 1950; Installation of the first of three pumps at the Town End Colliery, in an attempt to clear an underground lake, estimated to be 180ft deep, 4½ miles long and 2½ miles wide.

Compare this picture with the earlier views showing construction of the headframe. Note the middle pair of legs was absent until the sinking frame was dismantled. This headframe, at least by early 20th century standards, was exceptionally strong. The extra legs were necessary to withstand the forces generated by the weight of not only the triple deck cages being wound but also the steel ropes, each of which, each 2,600+ feet long, weighed nearly twenty tons.

This view reminds me of another more famous tower with steel fixed at all sorts of angles. It looks complicated but it is possible to construct something similar using plastic structural profiles, or take advantage of somebody else's labours and purchase an etched brass kit.

(opposite) The south face of the frame with corner plates galore.

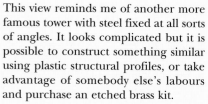

Coal Fact: In the 52 weeks ended 30th December 1961, some 110,559,000 tons of coal was transported by British Railways as against 22,115,000 tons by coastal shipping, 2,783,000 by canal, and 38,842,000 tons by road (including landsale).

This curved segment forms an archway with a similar section on the opposite side and strengthens the angle between one of the corner legs and the bottom cross member. The archway was necessary to give adequate clearance in the working area of the pithead for the movement of mine cars.

Coal Fact: Of the 7,836,000 tons of coal supplied to British Railways in 1961, it was made up by 6,000 tons of anthracite, 84,000 tons of slacks and smalls, 122,000 tons of graded coal, and 7,624,000 tons of large coal.

(opposite, bottom) The stairway allowing access to the upper levels of the headframe, is just visible in this view of the west side of the structure.

On the north side of the frame similar curved segments furthered the security of those legs.

Coal Fact: In 1961 the total amount of coal consumed by British Railways (mainly in locomotives) was 7,836,000 tons which had been supplied by all the NCB Divisions as follows; North Eastern (Yorkshire) 2,544,000 tons; South Western (South Wales) 1,338,000 tons; East Midlands (Nottinghamshire, Derbyshire, Leicestershire) 1,143,000 tons; Northern (Northumberland and Cumberland) 741,000 tons; Durham 621,000 tons; Scottish 587,000 tons; North Western (Lancashire., North Wales) 516,000 tons; West Midlands (Staffordshire, Warwickshire) 202,000 tons; South Eastern (Kent) 144,000 tons.

SNIBSTON COLLIERY - preservation in Leicestershire

We are fortunate indeed that a number of former colliery sites have been preserved. Most contain much of the infrastructure from the days when working coal mines existed in their hundreds. Snibston Colliery in Leicestershire is one such example and today the old mine forms the centrepiece of the Snibston Discovery Park. The following illustrations were captured during a visit in 2005, and show the preserved colliery very much as it was in 1983 when it closed. The area around Snibston was once thick with coal mines and some of the oldest pits inherited by the National Coal Board were located here. Snibston itself dates from the 1830's although many changes have happened since those early days when the railways themselves were in their infancy. Snibston is worth a visit.

(above) The upcast shaft/shafts headframe at Snibston was a tandem structure which, although unusual, was not unique and a small number of this type of headframe could be found around the British coalfields. Originally a timber structure, Snibston opened for business in 1835, this steel girder headframe was apparently erected in the 1930's.

(left) Another aspect of the tandem headframe of the upcast shafts at Snibston featuring the ventilation or fan house on the left. Note the huge exhaust pointing skywards, where the stale air from the mine was ventilation to air. The sheet metal enclosures around the shaft help create an airtight seal so that all the air sucked up by the fans went through the ventilation house. However, in practice, it was difficult to get a 100% seal on these shafts.

The north side of the tandem headframe showing more detail of the enclosures. Usually only men used the cages in these shafts to access the mine. All coal and most materials travelled in the downcast shaft where the air was sucked into the mine.

The more conventional downcast shaft headframe at Snibston. This is another rebuilt headframe using rolled steel girders. Markings on the girders show that they were made in Motherwell. This view, looking north-east, shows the mine car (tub) inclined creeper gantry, outlined in blue paint, which took the full tubs up to the bridge where they were turned and sent over the railway sidings to the coal disposal building.

The north aspect of the downcast headframe. The robust construction gives a clue to its daily roil of winding the cages full of coal tubs up and down the shaft. The brick building surrounding the pit head protected the personnel who worked on the surface here from the elements.

Coal Fact: In the three years from 1952 to the beginning of 1955, the NCB had built 19,000 new houses for miners at the new or reconstructed pits. This is about the same number as all the dwellings in the New Towns of Harlow and Crawley put up in the eleven years from 1947 to 1958.

A close-up of the girder construction of the stays which were substantial RSJ's with various cross bracing. Note the concrete foundations.

Coal Fact: April 1954; At the annual dinner of the East Midlands Section of the Institute of Fuel, held in Nottingham, Dr. A.Parker, Director of the Fuel Research Department, spoke on the possibilities of piping heat and energy from the depths of the earth when coal and oil resources became inadequate.

The down cast pit head at Snibston with the cage in position ready to unload its top deck. Although more than twenty years have passed since this working area was active, the museum has preserved much of the infrastructure so that visitors can observe just how the mine worked on the surface level. The cage doors would open so that tubs could be taken out of the cage and allowed, by gravity, to roll down the slight gradient to the creeper gantry where power would then take over. Empty tubs would enter the cage from the other side of the pit head floor to replace the 'fulls'. The cage would then be wound up so that the second level could be emptied and filled. Once the cage was loaded with empty tubs it would be wound down the shaft to the pit bottom for the reverse process to take place. Meanwhile another cage would have been wound to the surface to enable the surface process to take place again. And so it went on all day and all night. The only time that tubs were not brought up or taken back down was when were taken on board at the change of shift. note the cage guides depicted in blue paint.

Looking towards the pithead with the two sets of rails used to carry the tubs from the cages to the creeper gantry. Although not discernible here, there is a slight inclination downwards towards the camera.

Coal Fact: Phurnacite, one of the most popular of the domestic smokeless fuels available in Britain, was produced solely from a carbonised mixture of Welsh dry steam coal and pitch tar. It was one of the NCB's most profitable products, being manufactured at the former Powell Duffryn plant at Aberaman with sales reaching an all time high of 800,000 tons in 1973.

Looking towards the doorway where the rails intersected. Note the spacing of the metal sleepers set in concrete.

Coal Fact: 3rd May 1954; Coal merchants at Wallsend, Tyneside, staged a strike to protest against poor quality coal allocated to them for delivery to customers. They resumed deliveries on the 6th after meeting with the NCB.

(below) Now on the outside of the pithead building, we can see the rails joining at a spring loaded point. Some useful detail of the stays, stairway, railings and paint scheme can be gleaned from this view.

(left) Still on a falling gradient, the single set of rails now does a 180 degree turn to gain access to the creeper gantry where mechanical power took over. The tight radius was normal for these narrow gauge railways although no locomotives ever travelled these rails.

(below) The south-western corner of the winding house of the No.1, downcast shaft at Snibston. This is a typical design of winding house complete with arched multi-pane windows. Originally a bank of Lancashire boilers, situated in another building, provided the power for the large steam engine housed in this building but the NCB modernised the process so that electricity did the work.

One of the entrances to the winding house via a concrete stairway. Part of the original cast iron staircase can be seen on the west end of the building. The winding house was regarded as something of an inner sanctum, the man who worked there having one of the most important jobs in the whole mine. The seating is a museum addition.

Coal Fact: October 1946; The Minister of Food announced that the meat ration of underground miners would be increased by 75% from Sunday 3rd November.

The north-east corner of the winding house showing the 'working wall' where the wire winding ropes passed through the two openings from the winding drum to the sheaves.

Coal Fact: Private Owner coal wagons were still being built up to mid 1947, just six months before the railways were nationalised and some six months after the coal mines were nationalised. Although the P.O. coal wagon fleet was requisitioned by the Government at the beginning of World war Two, the wagons kept their previous identities as the intention was to hand them back to their original owners with the coming of peace.

The one-road engine shed at Snibston Colliery which, as can be seen, had a small extension added to the open, eastern end at an unknown date. The building is in good condition and today houses the preserved locomotives, both steam and diesel, which reside at the Snibston Discovery Park. Locomotives are steamed on specific dates and it would be advisable to enquire for opening times if further inspection of the building is required.

Coal Fact: January 1950; Brora coal mine in Sutherland, Scotland, the oldest in Britain, which was due to shut down in September 1949, was reprieved when a new company was formed to run it with an authorised capital of £5,000. Although the colliery was not in the 'big league' and produced only between 50 and 100 tons a week, it is memorable from the fact that coal was being dug there in the days of Mary Queen of Scots.

One of the ex-BR 16-ton mineral wagons which joined the NCB fleet and was actually treated to a full repaint at the time. Admitted, the livery in 2005 is somewhat lacking but much of the NCB colours and markings are still discernible. Note that this wagon had its original drop doors replaced by a fixed (welded) sheet. There are a large number of ex-BR mineral wagons on the Snibston site, most in the condition in which they worked for BR - requiring a repaint. Also on site are a number of mine cars of different shapes and sizes.

The completed 4mm scale Wrightscale headframe in all its glory. Malcolm will admit that this kit is certainly not for the beginner but with lots of patience, proper observance of the instructions and basic soldering skills you too can attain this standard of modelling which is an asset to any layout.

THE MODELS

In *Modelling Aspects of the Coal Industry* I mentioned briefly the **Wrightscale** colliery headframe kit which was then a fairly recent, and most welcome addition to the range of etched brass industrial modelling kits. Two years on and this volume covering *Further Aspects* is all the more richer by being able to include pictures of the **Wrightscale** headframe which have been kindly supplied by Malcolm and Sarah Wright. Further details of the availability of the etched brass kit can be gleaned later in this volume.

Besides the 4mm scale kit, Malcolm has also produced a 2mm scale model which is just as detailed as its larger cousin. Also available from **Wrightscale** for those of you who want to build their own headframe from whatever medium, but do not have either the skill or time to fabricate the wheels or sheaves, is a separate etched kit of the headframe sheaves as supplied in the headframe kit.

Different types of windows to suit both the colliery winding house and the screens (*see* diagram later) are further useful items which help to make architectural modelling easier.

Not content with producing all of the above, Malcolm Wright is now ready to release a kit for a non-working aerial ropeway which, even if you do not posses a colliery on your layout, can be sited anywhere to cross the railway out in the country to add a bit more realism above the embankment.

I would, at this point, like to thank Malcolm and Sarah for being so generous with their illustrations and information. Hopefully, their contribution to industrial modelling will continue.

Coal Fact: In 1722 the Tranent-Cockenzie wagon-way (laid with timber rails on stone blocks) was built to transport coal from mines at Tranent Moor to the harbour at Cockenzie, a distance of over 2$\frac{1}{2}$ miles. This first wagon way (or railway) in Scotland was situated some ten miles east of Edinburgh in an area called Preston Pans. An English company, the York Buildings Co. had been responsible for developing the coal pits, the harbour and the railway connecting them. The land itself, Tranent Estate, had been acquired from the forfeited estates of the Highlanders and on 21st September 1745 the wagon-way was the site of the Battle of Preston Pans when the opposing forces were drawn up on either side of the track, the Young Pretender, Bonny Prince Charlie on the east and the Royal troops on the west.

(*above*) Detail of the gallery situated approximately halfway up the stay legs. Based on the actual downcast headframe at Blaenant Colliery, the Wrightscale headframe could easily be adapted to follow another similar prototype, of which their were many, lattice girder type frame.

(*right*) The sheaves, or winding wheels, at the collieries used to wear out after a period of time and it was necessary to change them for new ones. This operation was usually carried out during the annual pit holiday when essential maintenance was carried out so that normal production was not disrupted. To make the wheel changing an easier process, many headframes had a hoist frame erected from simple h-section girders whereupon a hoist track was fixed. There was just enough clearance to left the wheel, slide the hoist along its track and, with the handrails removed, lower the old wheel prior to lifting a new one into position.

Coal Fact: The end of WW2 saw the Lanarkshire coalfield in central Scotland becoming exhausted but new coal mines were being developed in Fife during the late 1940s and early 1950s. This shift of production meant that the railways also had to move some of their operations and in 1956 a new marshalling yard, incorporating all the latest technology, was opened at Thornton to handle the output of the new collieries.

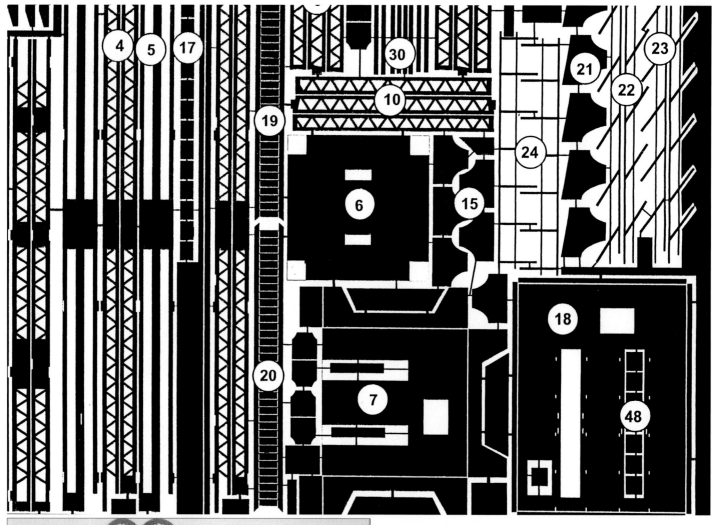

(above) A facsimile of a section of one of the 2mm scale etches as supplied by **Wrightscale** for their colliery headframe.

(left) The completed 2mm scale headframe reproduced here at nearly full size. The intricate nature of these lattice girder structures makes them appealing even to the non-modeller. It would seem a shame to hide the lower section of the main legs inside a pithead building.

Coal Fact: By the early 1870s Barnsley was recognised as the centre of Yorkshire coal mining and by 1874 it had 55 collieries producing 3.5 million tons per annum making it the most productive area in the country. The coal seam running under the area centred on Barnsley varied in thickness from 6ft to 11ft but was shallowest in the west and ran downwards as it progressed eastwards. Generally the coal seam became thicker as it went deeper. Therefore, by 1920 the centre of the Yorkshire coalfield had moved eastwards towards Doncaster as new technology enabled deeper mines to develop and tap the lower levels of the Barnsley seam on its eastern fringes.

Coal Fact: Having observed the eastward shift of the coal mines in Yorkshire during the late 1890s, the railway companies were quick to exploit the expected riches from the expanding coalfield. Gone were the days when any one company could guarantee to build a new line for its own purposes and most of the new lines built during the period, and into the early decades of the 20th century, were joint affairs with two or more partners. The new lines were promoted thick and fast and the turn of the century saw a minor 'Railway Mania' grip South Yorkshire. Each partner having equal rights to transport coal to nearby and distant markets.

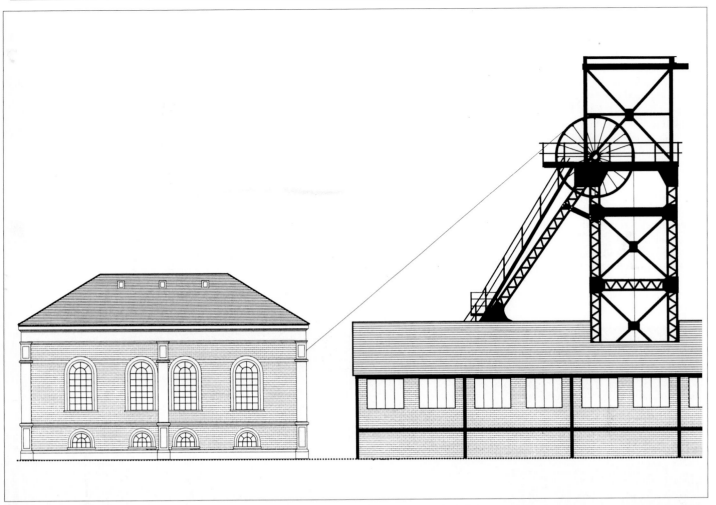

This part reproduction of the drawing supplied with the Wrightscale headframe kits, is included to show off the windows which are also available from Wrightscale. On the righthand building, and with a somewhat austere appearance, the frames used in the pithead and coal screening building are axact copies of those employed where inlaid brickwork forms the screen inside a girder frame. Literally hundreds of collieries had similar architecture. On the other hand, the winding house windows, and the walls too, had a somewhat grand style. Nevertheless, fabricating these particular windows can be taxing so now that they are available from Wrightscale don't waste any more time straining your eyes and nerves; someone has done it for you. With all the difficult parts of a colliery complex now commercially within your grasp, there is no need to wait any longer to recreate that eye-catching industrial diorama.

(below) Close-up of the landing showing the sheave mountings.

Coal Fact: The first use of conveyor belts in British mines, to carry coal from the face to the surface sizing screens, started in 1944 at Bullcliffe Wood, a small drift mine near Wakefield which was producing about 65,000 tons of coal a year. The conveyor belt concept had been proposed as long ago as 1905 but the expense was thought to be too great for large scale operation. By 1956 some 3,200 kilometres of conveyors had been installed in the main roadways of NCB mines and by 1980 more than 95 per cent of the coal moved underground was on conveyor belts.

Coal Fact: 17th July 1954; The 82nd pithead bath house to be built since the formation of the NCB, was opened at Pochin Colliery, Tredegar.

CWMAFON

Model Engineer Michael Edge has two well known 4mm scale layouts which he takes around the show circuit. The 27ft x 10ft CWMAFON layout, which is set in South Wales during the 1950-60's period, features a station, gravity sidings, steel works and a coal mine - Coed Cae Colliery. The theme of the layout is industrial and naturally Mike employs a number of the industrial locomotives which he produces in kit form for Judith Edge Kits, a business run by his wife Judith. Through the kind offices of Mike and Judith we are now going to have a quick tour of the colliery complex at CWMAFON which was created twenty-five years ago as one of the main components of the layout.

Including the pit head, washery, screens, spoil tip along with the associated sidings and spurs, the main part of the colliery section, measures approximately 9ft by 2ft. It straddles the main line via a tunnel and all parts are easily accessible to the operators. The colliery model is of a size which is impressive yet is not excessive in its size. Note there is only one headframe for instance - the second access could be a drift some distance away, off layout. However, the impression is there before your eyes - pleasing, functional and possible. The inventory of materials available to modellers nowadays is vast, with more and more manufacturers creating industrial 'bits' and 'pieces' which, when brought together with care and patience, can turn an idea or dream into a model to be both useful and proud of. Therefore such a model as is illustrated here is attainable by anyone who carefully plans the available space to create what is now a piece of British industrial history.

Mike's other layout, HERCULANEUM DOCK, also features aspects of the coal industry and is based on one of the coal exporting docks on the Mersey. However, the coal handling cranes, which tipped the wagon loads into ships holds, have yet to be built and full wagons are, at the moment, shunted offstage along the quayside.

Finally, I would like to thank Andy Ross who took many of the photographs which nicely capture this delightful model.

An overall view of Coed Cae Colliery showing the upper end of the screens with the dirt conveyor spanning the sidings and the headframe in the background. *Andy Ross.*

(opposite, top) Looking through the screens where the skeletal frame of the building is evident. *Andy Ross.*

(opposite) The other end of the screens with the dead-ended dirt bunker siding nearest. Being able to view the wagons beneath the screens is part of the pleasure of modelling one of these installations. Also, unless you are trying to depict an actual prototype colliery, you can customise the screens to any size and combination of roads which you desire. *Andy Ross.*

> **Coal Fact:** In 1949 the NCB had 4,116 shell (Lancashire type) boilers in use at its collieries, most of them hand fired. Another 522 boilers of the water tube type were also employed. All of these boilers together consumed 215,730 tons of coal a week at this time.

The lower section of the headframe with the preferred stairway, rather than ladders, climbing the structure. The 'steelwork' is built from brass section, with Plastruct used for handrails and the stairway. Stone and brickwork are, in the main, from the Slaters range. The attractive blue 'livery' was one of a number of different colour schemes used for headframes by the NCB. *Andy Ross.*

The reception end of the screens sidings with a number of empty 16-ton mineral wagons waiting to 'go under'. The newer concrete structure of the water circulator contrasts with the older brickwork of the screens and winding house. *Andy Ross.*

An overhead view of the colliery complex with the upcast shaft headframe nicely depicted in blue livery. To the right is the winding house which once housed a steam powered winding engine but is now home for quiet electric motors which drive the winding drums. Left of the headframe are conveyor bridges connecting the pithead with the screens and left of those can be seen a ventilation housing topped with an exhaust. The large roof section (removable to reveal machinery inside) covers the washery and screens, to its right and connected by a gantry, is the conical tower of the water circulator which cleans the water for recycling back into the coal washing process. *Andy Ross.*

The sidings at the upper end of the screens with wagons consisting mainly of the steel bodied 16-ton BR mineral variety. On the nearest track is a 24½-ton wagon which would normally not fit under these screens but modifications to the building has enabled these large modern wagons to be handled easily. However, the steelworks tippler cannot handle the 24½-ton wagons as they are too high to fit beneath the locking bar. So, whenever a train of these wagons is made-up they are taken as a block train to one of the fiddle yards for unloading. When these wagons were first introduced by BR, clearence problems forbade their use at many collieries and industrial customers until modifications were carried out. Notice part of the growing spoil tip bordering the sidings layout. *Andy Ross.*

A look at the construction and detail of the screens. Note the weathering taking its toll from the steel framework. Although the painters continually apply the brush, it is a thankless ongoing task in this dusty, dirty enviroment. Lighting adds another dimension to the model but don't get too carried away with illumination - the NCB didn't. *Andy Ross.*

Steam and diesel locomotives share the work at Coed Cae mine and off duty outside the engine shed are Ruston & Hornsby 0-6-0DE No.5, built from an MTK kit, and a scratchbuilt Hunslet 16inch 0-6-0ST. Note the elevated water tank which started life as a Cooper Craft road tanker but has now been put to much better use. *Andy Ross.*

Two of the NCB diesel locomotives shunt the screens. Left is a scratchbuilt Vanguard 0-6-0DH with a **J**udith **E**dge **K**its Sentinel 0-6-0DH nearest the camera. *Andy Ross.*

The **J**udith **E**dge **K**its six-coupled Sentinel lumbers beneath the dirt conveyor on its way back to shed. The bold blue and red livery of the diesel hydraulic is bespoke so you could have your locomotives in any combination of colour schemes. Brand new, the locomotive has yet to accumulate any weathering. Note the steel framework of the conveyor bridge which, even underneath, is nicely detailed and painted. *Andy Ross.*

North British Models Barclay 0-4-0ST, in the colours of its former owners - Cwmafon Iron & Steel Co. - is a recent NCB purchase for use at Coed Cae Colliery becoming No.6. Spotlessly clean, the engine is seen in the colliery yard adding further colour to the all blue local livery of the NCB fleet. The coal on the tank top shows that the engine has made an unofficial visit under the screens. Note the name JUDITH ANNE which was carried previously when the little tank was in CISC ownership and thoughtfully left in situ for its new employment. *Mike Edge.*

Coal Fact: January 1946; It was decided by the Football Association and Football League to consider the revival of the war-time embargo on mid-week cup ties, owing to absenteeism in the mining industry.

(left) The wagon tippler at the CISC steelworks with a 13-ton wagon being unloaded. Coal is tripped to the steelworks from the colliery by either NCB or CISC locomotives. Incidentally, the tippler can handle 21-ton wagons when necessary but the 24½-tonners are certainly prohibited. *Andy Ross.*

(below) The NCB Sentinel about to cross over the NCB bridge which spans the abandoned tracks of the former Alexandra Docks Railway on the lower level. *Andy Ross.*

A view of the screens from the tip. *Andy Ross.*

The massive stone built retaining wall hides the main line which passes beneath the colliery and lends a striking backdrop to the sidings on the lower level. *Andy Ross.*

WRIGHTSCALE

Burnside, Aboyne, Aberdeenshire, AB34 5ES.
Tel: 013398 86494.
Email: aboyne@abel.co.uk

Before Wrightscale introduced their 4mm scale colliery headframe kit in 2003, the British model market relied on either foreign imports, which usually needed major surgery to get them looking anything like the British prototype, or you scratchbuilt your own. Now, thanks to Malcolm Wright, you can construct your own British type colliery headframe from an etched brass kit in either 4mm or 2mm scale. Soldering is necessary but if you ever needed an excuse to take up the iron at last, then this is it. We look forward to many more mining orientated kits coming from Aboyne in the future but, in the meantime, make space for one of these superb models on your layout.

(above) A close-up of the completed 2mm headframe showing off the cable guards, or safety cage, on the mezzanine level.

(left) The Wrightscale 2mm scale colliery headframe with a one pound coin alongside for size comparison. Without a doubt this etched brass kit converts to an exquistite and highly deatailed model which is based on the headframe at Blaenant Colliery but the model has been selectively compressed so that it does not overbear its surroundings; nevertheless the completed structure stands a scale 65ft in height. This particular kit retails at about £50 (as at autumn 2005). The 4mm scale version is £108. Both kits come complete with scale drawings, and a booklet with not only assembly instructions included but also a lot of prototype information.

MANUFACTURERS, SUPPLIERS & SERVICES

(right) The top of the 4mm scale headframe with the sheaves, landing, mezzanine and hoist frame completing the assembly.

Probably the most difficult single item to fabticate when constructing a colliery headframe is the winding wheel or sheave. To make it even more of a task you needed two of them for each shaft/headframe and, if you work by the regulations, you need two mine shafts - by law. No wonder modellers never got around to making a natural addition to any model railway - a coal mine. However, somebody, somewhere was bound to come up with the answer and we must all thank our lucky stars that Malcolm Wright 'took the bit' and provided us with a scale model of a colliery winding wheel. We have, for years (decades it seems), been promised the wheels at least. Now we have it all and in different scales.

Support the manufacturers and they will come up with the goods.

(below) A facimile of a section of one of the three etched brass sheets found in the 4mm scale headframe kit. This shows some of the parts for building up the sheaves into their different layers. The availability of these particular sheaves as a separate item enables the scratchbuilder to complete his headframe too.

PARKSIDE DUNDAS

This company produce a superb range of coal industry related wagon kits in 2mm, 4mm and 7mm scales. Over the next two pages are a selection of the kits available in the relevant scales. The company usually display their range at something in excess of twenty model railway shows throughout the year, over the length and breadth of the country. However, if you cannot get to visit their stand you can contact them at:

PARKSIDE DUNDAS, Millie Street, Kirkcaldy, Fife, KY1 2NL.
Tel/Fax: 01592 640896.
Email: sales@parksidedundas.co.uk

2mm Scale Wagon Kits:

BR 24$\frac{1}{2}$-ton Mineral Wagon.
GWR 20-ton Coal Wagon (N24).
LMS 20-ton LOCO COAL Wagon.
LNER 20-ton LOCO COAL Wagon.

Simulated coal loads for the following manufacturers RTR hopper wagons:

Bachmann HEA/HSA, Minitrix HAA MGR.

Hopper tops for the Minitrix MGR hopper are also available.

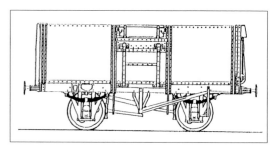

BR 16-ton Riveted body mineral wagon (Non Vacuum Diag. 109)

4mm Scale Wagon Kits:

BR 16-ton Mineral Wagon (Vacuum Fitted).
BR 16-ton Mineral Wagon (Non Vacuum Fitted).
BR 16-ton Mineral Wagon (ex French)(Cupboard style doors).
BR 16-ton Mineral Wagon (Sloping Sides).
BR 16-ton Mineral Wagon (Riveted Body & Non Vacuum Fitted).*
BR 21-ton Coal Wagon.
BR 21-ton Mineral Wagon: 1977 Rebuild.
BR 24$\frac{1}{2}$-ton Coal Wagon.
LNER 21-ton LOCO COAL Wagon (Steel Body).
RCH 1923 Pattern 5-Plank Mineral Wagon.
RCH 1923 Pattern 7-Plank 12-ton Coal Wagon.
RCH 1923 Pattern 7-Plank 12-ton Coal Wagon (Fixed Ends).
RCH (Sept.) 1923 Pattern 8-Plank 12-ton Coal Wagon.

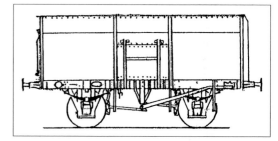

BR 16-ton Mineral wagon (Slope sides).

* The National Coal Board purchased hundreds of these particular '16 tonners' from BR in the 1960's.

Also available are Simulated Coal Loads for the following manufacturers RTR wagons:

Bachmann, Dapol, Hornby, Lima, Relica - Open Wagons.
Bachmann, Parkside Dundas - 16-ton Mineral Wagons.
Bachmann, Dapol, Replica - 24-ton Hopper.
Bachmann - MEA.
Hornby - 20/21-ton wagons.
Hornby - HAA MGR, Bachmann, Dapol, Replica - HBA/HEA.

BR 16-ton Mineral wagon
(Hand brakes only).

BR 24.5 ton Coal wagon

7mm Scale Wagon Kits:

BR 16-ton Mineral Wagon (Diagram 1/108).
BR 16-ton Mineral Wagon (Diagram 1/100) (ex Ministry of War Transport).
BR 16-ton Mineral Wagon (Diagram 1/112) (ex SNCF).
BR 21-ton Mineral Wagon (Diagram 1/107).
BR 24½-ton Mineral Wagon (Diagram 1/115).
GWR 20-ton 'Felix Pole' Coal Wagon (N23).
GWR 21-ton LOCO COAL Wagon (N28).
LMS 12-ton Open Wagon (Diagram 1667).
LNER (ex North British Railway) 'Jubilee' Coal Wagon.
LNER LOCO COAL Wagon (Diagram 77).
Private Owner Steel Chassis 13-ton Mineral Wagon.
RCH 1923 Pattern 7-Plank Mineral Wagon.
RCH 1923 Pattern 7-Plank Mineral Wagon (fixed ends).
RCH 1923 Pattern 8-Plank Mineral Wagon.

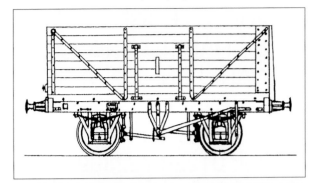

RCH (1923) 8-plank 12 ton Coal wagon.

7mm Scale Private Owner Wagon Kits (printed):

Based on LNER (exNBR) 'Jubilee' Coal Wagon Kit -

The Alloa Coal Company.
Balgonie Colliery.
R & J Burns.
Coltness Iron Company.
Cowdenbeath Coal Company.
J. & A. Davidson.
Devlin's Trawlers.
Ellis & McHardy.
Fife Coal Company.
Lochgelly Iron & Coal Company.
Lothian Coal Company.
James McAleer.
Moore.
Ormiston Coal Company.
Plean.
Smith Hood & Co. Ltd.
R.Taylor & Sons Ltd.
John Watson Ltd.
Wemyss Coal Company.
Wilsons & Clyde.
Woodhall Coal Company.

Standard **Parkside Dundas** 7mm scale BR 5-plank open wagon kit with added detail and moderate weathering as applied by The Wagon Works. *(photo TWW)*

Based on Railway Clearing House 1923 Pattern 7-Plank Mineral Wagon Kit -

Glasgow Iron & Steel Company.
Summers, Glasgow.

Based on BR (ex MofWT) 16-ton Mineral Wagon (Diagram 1/100) Kit -

Denaby.
Haunchwood.
Stewarts & Lloyds.

Based on Private Owner Steel Chassis 13-ton Mineral Wagon Kit -

J&J Charlesworth.
Fife Coal Company.
Stephenson Clarke.

Based on GWR 20-ton 'Felix Pole' Coal Wagon Kit -

Vale of Neath Colliery Co.

Also available are the following:

Transfers for BR Mineral Wagons in 1950's, 60's and 70's periods.
Transfers for Loco Coal Wagons in early and late LNER, and BR periods.

JUDITH EDGE KITS

JUDITH EDGE KITS
5 CHAPEL LANE
CARLTON
BARNSLEY
S71 3LE
Tel: 01226 722309
Email: edgemd@aol.com

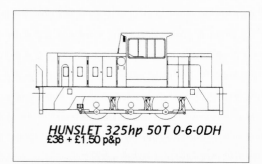

HUNSLET 325hp 50T 0-6-0DH
£38 + £1.50 p&p

This manufacturer has concentrated, in the main, on turning out industrial diesel locomotives although the range also covers LMS electric multiple units, Liverpool Overhead Railway coaching stock and other items of railway modelling interest. The industrials come in three separate scales, 3mm, 4mm and 7mm although 4mm dominates at the moment. On these few pages we illustrate outline drawings of the models appropriate to the coal industry which include diesel hydraulic and diesel mechanical types, including a couple of former British Railways classes. Before it became British Coal, the National Coal Board tended to standardise their diesel fleet and Sentinel diesel hydraulics became familiar at many pits. Likewise the 50 ton Hunslet 0-6-0DH. So the modeller is well catered for by Judith Edge Kits. Etched brass with a thickness of .015 inch is used for the kits. With a constantly growing range it is worth contacting JEK to inquire if your desired prototype is available yet. Kit building services are also available.

This beauty is a **J**udith **E**dge **K**its Hunslet 50-ton 0-6-0 diesel hydraulic recently built and supplied to a customer. It is finished as National Coal Board, N. Yorks Area No.44 which worked at Prince of Wales Colliery near Pontefract, and later at Royston Drift. *Mike Edge.*

The Hunslet fleet at the steelworks locomotive shed on the Cwmafon layout. Consisting 67-ton 0-6-0s, 80-ton 0-8-0s and a 1124 h.p. Bo-Bo. The two nearer locomotives are built from **J**udith **E**dge **K**its. *Andy Ross.*

A selection of other kits include -

4mm scale:

NBL/Paxman 0-4-0DH D2700-2
can be built as BR or industrial version
£42 + £1.50 p&p
NBL/Paxman 0-4-0DH D2703-7
£42 + £1.50 p&p
Hunslet 67 ton 0-6-0DH
£38 + £1.50 p&p
Barclay 0-4-0DM D2410-44
BR Class 06
£44 + £1.50 p&p
Barclay 0-6-0DM D2400-9
£38 + £1.50 p&p
LMS/BR Jackshaft drive
0-6-0DE 12023-32
£56 + £1.50 p&p

RUSTON 165DS 0-4-0DM D2957/8
£40 + £1.50 p&p

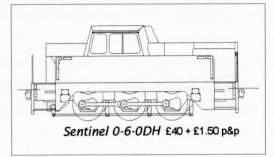

Sentinel 0-6-0DH £40 + £1.50 p&p

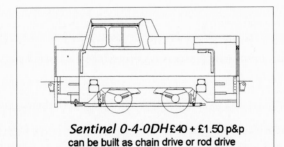

Sentinel 0-4-0DH £40 + £1.50 p&p
can be built as chain drive or rod drive

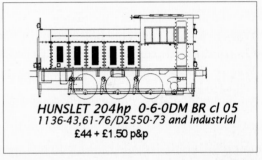

HUNSLET 204hp 0-6-0DM BR cl 05
1136-43,61-76/D2550-73 and industrial
£44 + £1.50 p&p

7mm scale:

Sentinel 0-6-0DH
£85 + £2.50 p&p
Hunslet 67 ton 0-6-0DH
£85 + £2.50 p&p
ES1 Bo-Bo
£120 + £2.50 p&p

3mm scale:

All at £38 + £1.50 p&p

Hunslet 67 ton 0-6-0DH
Sentinel 0-6-0DH
Ruston 165DS
NBL/Paxman 0-4-0DH

Cwmafon Iron & Steel Co. No.5, a Hunslet 67-ton 0-6-0DH. Although not one of the locomotive types employed by the National Coal Board, this is illustrated to show another of the models in the **J**udith **E**dge **K**its range. *Andy Ross.*

A pair of Parkside Dundas 12 ton 8-plank Southern Railway wagons with moderate weathering.

If you want a wagon kit putting together and then finishing to the highest standards just contact John Vincent at The Wagon Works. Fancy a whole batch of same company P.O. wagons or a load of BR mineral wagons in 7mm scale? On this and the opposite page we present a few of the various coal industry related wagons turned out by **The Wagon Works** at Sheffield. *(all illustrations by TWW.)*

This heavily weathered BR 20 ton riveted hopper, is another example of the superb kit building and excelent finish offered by **The Wagon Works** team. The wagon is built from a 7mm scale Piercey kit, distributed by DJH.

www.thewagonworks.co.uk

A pair of Piercey 20 ton hoppers, in British Railways and LNER livery. Both wagons have been subject to loads of additions and extreme weathering.

A Parkside Dundas 5-plank LMS open wagon which has received full weathering.

A Slaters 8-plank P.O. wagon in J.J.Charlesworth livery with added detail and moderate weathering.

DAVE BRADWELL   MODEL ENGINEER

Dave Bradwell, South Muirnich Cottage, Gorthleck, Inverness, IV2 6YP.

Tel: 01456 486377.   email d.bradwell@ukonline.co.uk

Dave Bradwell has several kits in his range that are relevant to the coal industry: All are for 4 mm scale.

BR 13 ton Hopper Wagon (left). This final design of 13 ton hopper for the BR fleet was built between 1949 and 1953. The kit uses etched brass as this is the ideal material to capture the appearance of these steel bodied vehicles.
14 ton Steel Hopper Wagon (right). This design by Charles Roberts was built for private concerns, particularly the NCB, from the 1950s and was probably the basis for the BR type alongside. The kit again in etched brass, reflects the differences in brake and other details from the BR wagon. The NCB legend is a Modelmasters decal. The kits do not include wire, castings or wheels. The etched underframes include springing - this is much easier to arrange than compensation in this type of wagon. Price as at 2005 is £12 each. Add £1 postage per order in UK.

21 ton Hopper Detailing Etch. Etched brass parts to upgrade four (4) ready-to-run models. Includes end platforms, steps, batter plates, bottom door handles, handrail supports and one full chassis with correct high level brake to match the riveted bodies. Price - £6 each, or 5 for £25. Shown above are three Hornby (ex-Dapol) 21 ton hoppers with added detail using the etched parts. The wagon on the right has the replacement underframe with high brake lever and new brakes.

Please check availability and prices before ordering.

We also have a range of 4mm scale highly detailed etched locomotive and tender kits.

Website - www.davebradwell.co.uk

MODEL BUILDINGS

Peter Smith at Kirtley Model Buildings specialises in 1/43rd scale and besides the architectural models he can also create the trackwork for a mine complex or any part of a colliery at any period. All he requires are a few photographs or photoopies and, if possible, a rough or photocopied plan of your requirements. You can contact him either by post at:

47 Kestrel Road, Melton Mowbray, Leicestershire, LE13 0AY *or call:*

Workshop & Fax - 01664 853142; Home - 01664 857805 *or E-Mail:*

kirtleymodels@ntlworld.com

He will get in touch to discuss your ideas, and to give an initial quote. If you decide to proceed, a detailed specification will be worked out, and a firm price agreed on.

2mm Scale (N Gauge) RTR Quality Line Wagons:

10ft Wheelbase:

Coal 7-Plank GWR.
Coal 7-Plank LMS.
Coal 7-Plank LNER.
Coal 7-Plank SR.
Coal Butterley Steel Type BR.
Coal Butterley Steel Type GW.
Coal Butterley Steel Type NE.
Mineral 5-Plank GWR.
Mineral 5-Plank LMS.
Mineral 5-Plank LNER.
Mineral 5-Plank SR.

Private Owner Wagons 5-Plank:

John Allbutt
Stevenson.

Private Owner Wagons 7-Plank:

Ammanford.
Chatterley Whitfield.
Crigglestone.
Lydney.
Norchard.
Parkend.
Princess Royal.
Tredegar.

Butterley Steel Type:

Charrington.

Modern Rolling Stock:

BR MGR Coal Hopper Wagon - Pre-TOPS 'HOP AB'.
BR MGR Coal Hopper Wagon - Tops 'HAA' Railfreight.

PECO

Railway Models

A long standing name in the model railway world, Peco has a number of wagons in 2mm, 4mm and 7mm scale suitable for coal industry employment on your layout. Available in most model shops, items can be got direct from:
**Peco Railway Models, Beer, Seaton, Devon, EX12 3NA.
Tel: 01297 21542 - Fax: 01297 20229.**

2mm Scale Wagon Kits - 9ft Wheelbase:

BR 16-ton Steel Mineral Wagon.
7-Plank Open Wagon.

Also available are Coke Extension Boards to fit 7-Plank wagons.

4mm Wagon Body Cards - 7-Plank Coal, Clean Finish:

Baddesley.
Hood & Son.
Kingsbury.
Pinxton.

4mm Wagon Body Cards - 7-Plank Coal, Weathered Finish:

Anderson & Co.
Emlyn.
Moseley.

Also available are Coke Extension Boards to fit 7-Plank wagons.

7mm Wagon Kits:

BR 16-ton Mineral Wagon.

Further recommended reading:

A LANCASHIRE TRIANGLE Part One	D.J.Sweeney	Triangle Publishing
A LANCASHIRE TRIANGLE Part Two	D.J.Sweeney	Triangle Publishing.
THE INDUSTRIAL RLYS OF BOLTON, BURY		
AND THE MANCHESTER COALFIELDS Vol.1&2	Townley, Peden et al	Runpast.
THE 4mm COAL WAGON	J.Hayes	Wild Swan.
INDUSTRIAL & MECHANISED MODELLING	D.Rowe	Wild Swan.
ARCHITECTURAL MODELLING in 4mm Scale	D.Rowe	Wild Swan.
LANDSCAPE MODELLING	B.Norman	Wild Swan.
THE ART OF WEATHERING	M.Welch	Wild Swan.

Another list of recommended books can be found on the last page of *Modelling Aspects of the Coal Industry,* whereupon there is a list of sources which have also been consulted for both volumes.

ACKNOWLEDGEMENTS

Putting this second volume together has been a pleasurable and, once again, an enlightening experience. It is heartening to realise that all of the people and the various organisations which I approached, were nothing less than helpful. Everybody responded positively.

David Allen of Book Law Publications was both supportive and enthusiastic towards this second helping and I would like to thank his family, including Hazel, Jackie, Kath and Chris, for looking after me during my numerous visits to Nottinghamshire.

Horace Gamble loaned a large number of industrial locomotive photographs of his own taking so that I could make my final selection at home. The results of Horace's many visits to industrial sites during the 60's and 70's, have helped enormously to illustrate this volume. Thank you Horace.

In search of steam motive power, Malcolm Castledine was one of those railway photographers' who branched out into the realms of the industrial railway systems when BR steam became extinct. Malcolm managed to make a number of visits to the north-east of England where he recorded the last days of steam working on the National Coal Board lines and some of the images he captured on film appear within.

The modelling fraternity or to be more exact the model engineers who create the kits which we put together, are, because of their skills, another breed seemingly apart from us lesser mortals but, they are not only approachable, they are also very helpful and I must thank Dave Bradwell, Mike and Judith Edge, John Vincent, and Malcolm and Sarah Wright. Other people I would like to thank include Bob Bruce, Eric Fry, Graham Hooper, Roy Sheffield, Cliff Shepherd, Roy Shipley, Neville Stead, Ken Swainson, and Richard Walls.

Relevant organisations and some of the individuals concerned with them also helped contribute towards the completion of this book and are as follows: The Red Rose Steam Society; members of the Industrial Railway Society; Stuart Oliver (RJB); Alan Davies; Anna Siddall; Steve Kee; Leicestershire County Council; National Mining Museum of England; UK Coal (formerly RJB Mining) - Thank you all.

And finally!...........

Private sector corporate identity has brought a touch of colour and variety to the modern day railway scene in Britain. This is a National Power Class 59, No.201, with a train of 102 tonne coal hoppers - the 21st Century merry-go-round which is rapidly superseding the 1960's design HAA m.g.r. trains which in their day revolutionised the movement of coal on BR. The 'modern' railway scene and its association with the coal industry from a modelling point of view, will be the subject of another book in the making for future publication. If you can contribute any illustrations (b/w or colour, photographs or slides) maps, plans/elevations of coal related transport or installations from the mid-1960's to date, for this forthcoming title, then please contact the author via the publisher. Photograph - *Ken Swain.*